~ Table of Contents ~

Introduction to Adulting 5

Part One: What You Should Know About Personal Finance 9

    Opening a Bank Account 11

    Understanding Your Paycheck 17

    Creating a Personal Budget 23

    What Is Credit and What Building Credit Means For Your Future 29

    The Importance of Saving 35

    Using Student Loans 41

    Getting a Car Loan 47

    The Basics of Doing Taxes 53

    Stock Market Basics 59

    Various Kinds of Insurance and How to Get Them 65

    Retirement Accounts 71

    Reading a Financial Statement 77

    Making a Good Impression 83

    How To Talk To My Parents About Finances 87

Part Two: Something for Everyone 89

    Introducing the Buckets, Shovels, Beach and Map 90

    The Shovels Working Together 97

Part Three: Building Your Own Plan 99

Copyright © 2019 by Stephen D. Mayer

All rights reserved. No part of this publication may be reproduced, distributed, or transmitted in any form or by any means, including photocopying, recording, or other electronic or mechanical methods, without the prior written permission of the publisher, except in the case of brief quotations embodied in critical reviews and certain other noncommercial uses permitted by copyright law. For permission requests, write to the publisher, addressed "Attention: Permissions Coordinator," at the address below.

SD Mayer & Associates LLP
235 Montgomery Street, 30th Floor
San Francisco, CA 94104
(415) 691-4040
www.sdmayer.com

Ordering Information:
Quantity sales. Special discounts are available on quantity purchases by corporations, associations, and others. For details, contact the publisher at the address above. Orders by U.S. trade bookstores and wholesalers. Please contact the publisher at the address above.

Printed in the United States of America

DISCLAIMER:
All calculations and data presented within SD Mayer & Associates LLP publications and digital marketing and media including but not limited to websites, brochures, presentations and return models are deemed to be accurate, but accuracy is not guaranteed. The projected pro forma returns on investment are intended for the purpose of illustrative projections to facilitate analysis and are not guaranteed by SD Mayer & Associates LLP or its affiliates and subsidiaries. Past performance is not an indicator of future results.

The information provided herein is not intended to replace or serve as a substitute for any legal, real estate, tax, or other professional advice, consultation or service.

INVESTMENT RISKS:
All investments, including real estate, is speculative in nature and involves substantial risk of loss. We encourage our investors to invest carefully. We also encourage investors to get personal advice from your professional investment advisor and to make independent investigations before acting on information that we publish. Much of our information is derived directly from information published by companies or submitted to governmental agencies on which we believe are reliable, but are without our independent verification. Therefore, we cannot assure you that the information is accurate or complete. We do not in any way warrant or guarantee the success of any action you take in reliance on our statements or recommendations.

Past performance is not necessarily indicative of future results. All investments carry risk and all investment decisions of an individual remain the responsibility of that individual. There is no guarantee that systems, indicators, or signals will result in profits or that they will not result in losses. All investors are advised to fully understand all risks associated with any kind of investing they choose to do. Hypothetical or simulated performance is not indicative of future results. Unless specifically noted otherwise, all return examples provided in our websites and publications are based on hypothetical or simulated investing. We make no representations or warranties that any investor will, or is likely to, achieve profits similar to those shown, because hypothetical or simulated performance is not necessarily indicative of future results. Don't enter any investment without fully understanding the worst-case scenarios of that investment.

~ Introduction to Adulting ~

After writing the book, *5 Buckets, 4 Shovels, a Beach and a Map*, and giving it to clients and friends, I found something interesting happened—they shared it with their kids. That book uses pictures and easy-to-understand concepts to explain financial planning. Five buckets represent asset categories for allocating personal wealth, and four shovels represent the four typical financial advisors needed to make wise spending and saving decisions. I had been using analogies like buckets and shovels for more than 40 years with my own clients to help them develop their financial plans. So when we published the book, it was both fascinating and exciting to discover its value to a younger audience.

With that in mind, I began thinking about all of the basic personal finance topics that young adults should know as they enter adulthood—topics that aren't being taught in school. These are concepts that my parents taught me as a teenager but that a lot of kids don't know about today. For example, how do you open a bank account? When I was five-years-old, my dad drove me down to the local Police Credit Union, walked me through the process of opening my first bank account, and explained how it would help me. Today, instead of driving down to the local bank, you can use a mobile device to research whatever you need to know about opening an account—and then apply online. At the end of the day, regardless of how you do it, you'll still end up with a bank account.

In this book, we try to focus on the concepts, why it's important to know this stuff, and how to make it work for you. We understand that there are a variety of ways to put the concepts into practice, whether you speak to a human being or do everything on your mobile device; but the important part is understanding the back story—the reason why financial planning is so important.

Each chapter is broken down into five components: Why Do I Need To Know This?, How Do I Get Started?, Quick Tips, Personal Finance Stories, and Exercises. The idea is to give you a few ways to digest the information, provide some quick tips to get you started, describe a real-life scenario putting the topic into action, and give you a practice exercise using your own information to be sure you understand the concept in each chapter.

I hope this book will be useful and that someday you'll be able to sit down with your children and explain these concepts to them, regardless of the tools they are using—like a chip embedded in their brains instead of the mini-computer you once carried in your pocket.

On a personal note, I want to thank all those involved with the creation of this second book. The marketing team at my firm, SD Mayer & Associates, helped write and produce this book, including Greg Barber, Yasi Agah, and a team of marketing interns. Thank you to Amy Sparkman for editing our book and for her invaluable input. I also got plenty of feedback and support from my kids, who are young adults themselves—Dylan, Kenzie and Nicola, and from my wife, Patty Mayer. Finally, Rich Sigberman drew all of the illustrations, which helped bring the concepts to life.

This book has been donated through the tremendous support of our friends and corporate sponsors, whose financial contributions to our 5 Buckets, 4 Shovels Foundation made this all possible. The mission of the foundation is to use the proceeds from the sale of our other books, "5 Buckets, 4 Shovels, a Beach and a Map" and "The Toughest Guy I Ever Knew and Other Short Stories," to be used to support financial literacy for young adults in high school and college. The proceeds are used to purchase these books, and the goal is to reach one million young adults within five years.

All of my books are available for purchase on amazon.com or through our local San Francisco Bay Area chain of bookstores, Books, Inc. or through our website, 5buckets4shovels.com.

Adulting

Adulting (v): to do grown up things and hold responsibilities such as, a **9-5** job, a **mortgage**/rent, a car **payment**, or anything else that makes one think of grown ups.

Source: UrbanDictionary.com

~ Part One: What You Should Know About Personal Finance ~

So, what are the financial topics that you should know about? As a young adult, you should have a general understanding of bank accounts, your paycheck, budgeting, credit, and debt, savings, loans, taxes, the stock market, and retirement. There are a couple of extra chapters about financial statements, which is a more advanced topic, and some tips on how to make a good lasting impression, which is a definite key to success.

There is a lot to know! Our goal is to give you enough information for you to be able to put the concepts of personal finance to use in your own life. Some people spend their whole careers specializing in just one of these topics—it's hard to become an expert in any of them! If they seem confusing, don't worry. This book will explain the basics, and the basics will give you a good foundation to build on as you grow in experience and financial independence. Now, let's get started.

Opening a bank account

Why Do I Need one?

Banks can be a hassle—especially when you factor in all the fees—first, to open a bank account; second, to use certain ATMs; third, if you overdraft, that is, spend more money than you have in your account. Plus, bank hours are not always convenient. But, banks are an essential part of life. You might have been told that it's too risky to keep a lot of money in your house—what if there's a fire or earthquake? And carrying around wads of cash makes you an easy target to rob. More important is the fact that you want your money to work for you! Money in a bank account makes it easier to make purchases in stores and online; it can earn a little interest (more on that topic later); it can even give you a reputation (hopefully a good one!).

When your money is in a bank, the Federal Deposit Insurance Corporation (known as the FDIC) automatically protects it, up to $250,000. When you get a job, you can have your paycheck automatically deposited into your bank account, which means you'll never lose it or spend the money too quickly. A bank account comes with an ATM card, which you can use to withdraw money at any time to pay for gas, food, a movie—just about anything.

How Do I Get Started?

Opening your first bank account is a big deal. It means you're ready to be responsible for your own money—for how much you spend AND how much you save. You're starting down the path to financial independence. The first

Quick Tips

- If you'll be doing most of your banking online and using your ATM card a lot, make sure that the bank you choose is set up for that and won't be charging you fees for excess use.

- Some savings accounts limit the number of times you can transfer money through an app.

- For higher interest rates, credit unions can be a good banking choice. They'll usually give you the best rates and still offer all of the advantages of one of the bigger banks.

- Online-only banks are also an option, but make sure you do your research, to make sure you have access to your money when you need it and can speak to someone if you need assistance.

step is to choose a bank. Talk to your parents or guardians. Find out which bank they use and ask them what they like and don't like about the services it offers. Visit a few of the banks in your town or city. You're likely to do most of your banking online or on your smartphone. But sometimes you need to visit the actual bank for assistance, so you want to choose one that's easy to get to and open at times when you can get there.

It's important to find out what you need to open an account ahead of time. Different banks have different qualifications. For instance, most banks require a parent or guardian's signature on the account if you're under 18. You'll definitely need an identification card, like a driver's license or passport. And you'll need all of your personal information: birthdate, home address, and social security number. Being prepared makes a big difference—it shows the bank that you're responsible and ready for this step!

Next up is a trip to the bank you've chosen! Once you go to the bank, you'll meet with a banker to open your account. There are some banks that let you open an account online or over the phone, but doing it in person is a great way for a first time user.

Your first decision is to choose the type of account you want. Typically, the choice is either a checking or a savings account—or both. A checking account is used for everyday purchases, such as gas, food, shopping or anything else you need or want to buy. A savings account is exactly what it sounds like: a place to save your money rather than spend it. Many people put a certain amount from their paycheck into their savings account each week or month. A savings account is what you'll draw on for large purchases (like a car or a computer), for emergencies, or for retirement.

Based on your research before you went to the bank, you should have brought with you the necessary information and the money needed to open your account—your first deposit.

Once your banker has opened the account for you, be sure to ask any questions. For instance, be sure you understand any fees the bank charges when you withdraw money, or when your balance is too low. You'll definitely want

Personal Finance Stories

Evan got his first job at age 16, mowing lawns and helping his parents' friends around the neighborhood. They all paid him in cash, which he kept in an envelope in his dresser drawer and used as spending money when he went out with his friends. It wasn't a lot of money, so he didn't really need a bank account at the time.

Fast forward a year, Evan is now 17, working part-time at the local pet store. The company pays him a regular paycheck, which he has to cash out for spending money. His parents also advised him to save a little from each paycheck to save for the car he plans to buy by the end of the year. As an incentive, they offered to match whatever he can save.

Evan went online and found a website that describes all of the online banking options, as well as reviews by users and some of the pros and cons of each. Ultimately, he chose a bank that provided access to a worldwide network of ATMs, had no transaction fees, a good mobile banking app, and a pretty good interest rate on his savings account. Set up was easy, and now he's already started saving for the car he wants.

Exercise: Writing & Understanding a Check

Sometimes You Need To Write A Check

Although 99% of what you purchase can be paid over your phone, online or through an app, there will be times when you will have to write a check. There is also information on your checks that will help when you want to put down a deposit on a vehicle or may car payments.

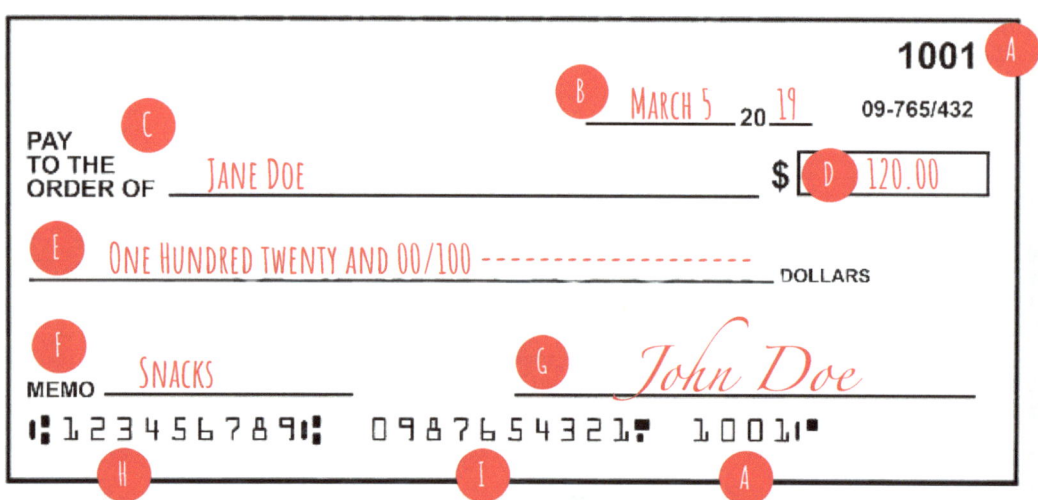

Exercise: Identifying Parts of a Check

- **A** Check Number
- **B** Date
- **C** Name of Person Being Paid
- **D** Dollar Amount Being Paid (Numerals)
- **E** Dollar Amount Being Paid (Written)
- **F** Memo (Optional Notes)
- **G** Your Signature
- **H** Routing Number
- **I** Bank Account Number

to know the maximum number of withdrawals you can make in a month. If you have a savings account, you'll want to know the current interest rate. Your banker will answer any question you have—and you can always stop by another day if a new questions comes up. In the meantime, you are done—you now have a bank account in your name with your own money in it!

Now comes the fun part—setting up your mobile banking app. That's where you'll do most of your banking, including depositing checks, making online payments, checking statements, and making transfers.

Understanding Your Paycheck

Why Do I Need To Know This?

At some point, you are going to get a job. In exchange for your hard work, you receive a paycheck. Believe me, you're going to want to understand everything about it. Consider this: You get your first job and you're going to make $10 per hour and work 20 hours a week. Simple math tells you that in one week you should make $200. But when you get your paycheck, it says that you only made $130. What happened to the other $70?

How Do I Get Started?

The first step is to get a job! Perhaps you've been putting it off, but now you're ready to take the leap, to earn some money and take one more step toward financial independence. Let's assume you're the person in the example above: you're going to make $10 per hour and work 20 hours a week. That means your gross income (the amount you earn before taxes are taken out) will be $200 per week.

The next step is to fill out forms that you're new employer will give you on your first day of work. One of these forms is called a W-4, which is where you record the number of "allowances" you want to take. Let's assume that you're a full time student, you're unmarried and have no children. You'll want to list 0 or maybe 1 allowance so that the maximum amount of money is withheld from your paycheck each pay period. The money that's withheld covers your federal taxes. The more allowances you take, the less money that's withheld. BUT, the less money that's withheld now, the more likely you'll owe money to the government at the end of the year. That's not a good idea!

Quick Tips

- Always keep track of the hours you work.
- Check your paycheck to make sure you are being paid fairly. Report any mistakes to your manager.
- Keep your paystubs safe—often your personal information is listed on them like your social security number, address or phone number.
- At the end of the year, you'll get a summary of your paychecks called a W-2, which you'll use for your taxes.
- Based on how much you make, you should try to put a certain amount, like 10%, in your savings account. An ideal savings account will have 6 months of pay.

Claiming zero allowances means the maximum amount of taxes are taken out of each paycheck, and it's likely you'll get a refund at tax time. Now let's learn more about taxes.

Federal and State Taxes

Everyone has federal taxes taken from their paychecks. That's the first slice of the pie you'll see missing. You can adjust how much is taken out by changing the number of allowances you enter on the W-4 form when you first get hired.

State taxes are a different story. Depending on where you live, you may or may not have to pay state income tax. If you live in a state that collects taxes, you'll see a line item for state tax on your paycheck—another piece of the pie.

Social Security

The federal government requires that every working person contributes to social security, which is a fund that provides supplemental retirement income to all people over the age of 65. The amount each person receives is based on the amount of money the person has earned over his or her lifetime. Social security funds are calculated to be 6.2% of each person's total gross income, and it's distributed monthly until death.

Medicare

Along with social security, the federal government requires every working person to contribute to Medicare, which is a government provided insurance plan that pays for hospital, medical, and surgical benefits for people who are 65 years old and older, and for some people with disabilities. This contribution amounts to 1.45% of your gross income.

Workers' Compensation/Disability

These are contributions to a tax funded program that provides support in the event that you are injured or disabled on the job and are unable to work for a period of time.

Unemployment

These deductions provide financial support in the event that you are laid off or lose your job due to no fault of your own. In other words, if you get fired for stealing paperclips, you can't get unemployment payments.

Personal Finance Stories

Reggie finally got his first job. At the interview, he was told he'd be paid $10 per hour and would work between 16-20 hours per week. He was excited at the thought of earning his own money and being able to pay for entertainment, clothing and a few other things. He would be paid every other week.

After two weeks of working at the coffee shop, he totalled 36 hours. By his calculations, his first paycheck would be for $360. On payday, his boss handed him his paycheck, and he ripped it open to find that it totalled $290. Confused, he told his boss that there must have been a mistake. His his boss laughed and told him that Uncle Sam took his cut.

Still confused, Reggie went home and asked his parents if they knew Uncle Sam. They certainly did! Reggie's parents explained that for every dollar he earns, a small percentage gets taken out for taxes, which pays for things like federal and state programs, social security, unemployment insurance, etc. Reggie didn't think it was fair, but his parents said that it's just the way it is - that the money goes to help other people, and someday, once he old enough, he might need to use those programs for himself.

Other Deductions

Your employer might deduct other things from your paycheck, such as the following:

- If your employer offers medical, dental, and vision benefits, you might see deductions for your employer-sponsored plans. Typically, it's a shared cost, where you and the company contribute a portion every paycheck

- Also, if your employer offers a retirement plan, your contributions to your retirement plan might appear on your paycheck. This money is going into a savings account for your future use, which is a good thing.

- Finally, there are a variety of other items you might see, like a Flexible Spending Account or a Health Savings Account. These are accounts that use pre-tax dollars to pay for health insurance co-payments, or to cover medical expenses. Typically, these aren't offered to young people—not until you're out of school and entering the world of full-time work.

Altogether, that's a lot of money coming out of your paycheck well before you cash it! And that's why we wanted to make sure you aren't surprised when you see your first one. Be sure you review each paycheck carefully, check for any errors, and, if you find any, let your employer know immediately so it can be corrected.

Finally, keep your paystubs safe. They usually contain your address, social security number, and full name on them, which you don't want falling into the wrong hands. Tossing them into the glove box is not as safe as sticking them in a locked drawer or filing cabinet inside your house. Be wise. Be responsible. And enjoy earning your own money!

Exercise: Reading a Paycheck

What You See Isn't Always What You'll Get

PAYCHECK

Check Date: 03/05/2019 **Company #:** 12334567890 **PTO Balance:** 5 Hours
Period Begin: 02/16/2019 **Check #:** 10527
Period End: 02/28/2019 **Employee #:** 33
Hire Date: 06/05/2017 **Net Pay:** 333.20

EARNINGS

Description	Rate	Hrs	Current	Year To Date
Regular	11.00	33.51	368.81	2,337.70
Overtime			0.00	16.22
Total Earnings		33.51	368.61	2,353.92
Total Direct Deposit				

DEDUCTIONS

Description	Current	Year To Date
Federal	3.53	68.73
Social Security	22.85	145.94
Medicare	5.34	34.13
CA State	0.00	0.24
CA SDI	3.69	23.54
Total Deductions	35.41	272.58
Check Amount	333.20	2,081.34

Exercise: Getting To Know Your Paycheck

Quiz yourself to see how well you understand what a paycheck tells you:

1. How much does this person make per hour?
2. How many hours did this person work during the pay period?
3. How much did this person earn during the pay period?
4. How much did this person get paid for this pay period?

Creating a personal budget

Why Do I Need To Know This?

A budget helps you keep track of your spending, pay your bills, and save up for the things you want. Whether you make just a little bit of money or a whole lot, having a budget is a good way to divide your paycheck up into categories so that you don't overspend As a young adult, you might not have too many financial obligations other than buying food when you go out or going to the movies. But as you get older, you might have a car payment, car insurance, and gas to pay for, along with new clothes and school supplies. Knowing how much money is coming in and what you planning what spend it on each month can help prevent you from running out of money before you receive your next paycheck.

How Do I Get Started?

In the first chapter, you set up a bank account to store your money. Now you're ready to spend it. Not so fast! First, let's learn about this beautiful financial tool we call budgeting.

Budgeting is a financial plan for a particular period of time, such as one year. A budget enables you to keep track of how much money you make and how much you spend, and to ensure you'll have enough money to cover all your necessary purchases.

Quick Tips

- Use a mobile app that will automatically categorize your spending and download information from your bank and credit card company. This kind of app can help you track your spending, set spending limits by category and send you notifications if you spend a little too much.

- Overspending can lower your credit score, which is NOT a good thing. There are serious advantages to having a high credit score! More on that in an upcoming chapter.

- Check your budget at least once a week to make sure you're on track. You don't want your ATM card being declined because you're out of money. Your mobile banking app should have a budgeting tool. Use it!

We begin by looking at your bank statement for the last month. You can usually find these bank statements online through your bank's website. What have you spent money on? How much have you spent on food, like at restaurants or coffee shops, esports, gaming, clothing, jewelry or gas? Can you see where you can save money?

These are the questions you want to ask yourself as you look through your bank statement. In a notebook or on your computer, list the spending categories that pertain to your everyday life, such as food, books, clothes, and gas. Under each category, list the average amount you spent this month. Then add all the average amounts together to find the total amount of money you spent last month. What does the amount tell you about your spending habits? What do you buy most often? What do you spend the least on?

Now, take a look at how much you add to your bank account each month. Whether it's an allowance, a gift or a paycheck, make sure to add it all together and write down your total income next to the total amount you spent last month. You can tell a lot from comparing those two numbers. Based on what you see, you'll be able to decide whether or not to change your monthly spending habits.

So your monthly budget shows the income you deposit into your account and the money you withdraw from that account by category. A good budget is balanced! In other words, you don't spend more than you make. A really good budget also saves a little each month, getting you to financial independence more quickly.

You can keep track of your budget in a notebook, on your computer, or through an app. Using online banking tools is especially helpful because they can be linked to your bank account, which will help you track and categorize all your spending. They'll also tell you when you're spending too much. Look online for "budgeting tools," and decide which one is the right tool for you.

Personal Finance Stories

Katie loves to shop…a lot. Champagne taste on a beer budget is what it's called. She makes about $500 per week working at a local clothing store, but about $100 per paycheck goes straight back to taxes. Her parents gave her their old car when she went off to college, but she has to pay for gas, which costs about $40 per week. Her clothing addiction costs her about $200-300 per month, and she likes to show off her new outfits by going out with friends. Her entertainment and dining costs are about $300 per month. She has a credit card, which is costing her about $100 per month. Miscellaneous expenses are about $150 per month. If you do the math, you'll quickly see that Katie is overspending.

Her parents were helping Katie by sending her money each month for school expenses, but have recently they told her that she needs to cut back on her spending. She downloaded an app on her phone that allows her to enter all of her bank accounts and credit cards, and then tracks her spending by category. The app automatically updates her balances and sends her texts when she's near her limit. Using the app, Katie has learned to skip a few non-essential lattes, cut out a couple of new outfits, eat "in" more often, and still enjoy life! The hardest part was just getting everything set up; now she can't live without it.

Exercise: Building a Budget

It's All About Living Within Your Means

"Living within your means" just means that you don't spend more than you earn so you don't run out of money before your next paycheck. In our paycheck chapter, we earned a little over $600 per month, so that's all we can spend every month on food, entertainment, clothing, and other expenses, like gas.

Budgeting is just the exercise of estimating how much your lifestyle will cost you and then not spending more than what you make. Hopefully you won't spend it all so you can put some toward your savings account.

Let's give budgeting a shot using your own information.

MONTHLY BUDGET

INCOME	Monthly Budget	Actual Amount	Difference
Income (Paycheck, Allowance, Birthday Money, etc.)			
Interest Income (Savings Account)			
INCOME SUBTOTAL			

EXPENSES	Monthly Budget	Actual Amount	Difference
Money To Savings			
Bills			
Rent/Mortgage			
Utilities/Cell Phone			
Groceries/Snacks			
Car			
Car Payment			
Car Insurance			
Gas			
Entertainment (Movies, Pizza, Video Games, Bowling)			
Other Expenses			
EXPENSE SUBTOTAL			
NET INCOME (Income minus Expenses)			

What credit is and what building credit means for your future

Why Do I Need To Know This?

Saving enough money to make a big purchase can take a long time—too long if your purchase will make a big difference in your lifestyle. Wouldn't it be awesome to be able to drive to work yourself and save the time and frustration of walking or taking public transportation? But even a used vehicle costs a lot of money, and saving to buy one can take months, even years.

But there's a solution: buying on credit. This means you borrow the money you need and agree to pay that money back on a pre-arranged schedule over a set period of time. Usually, you will be charged a monthly fee, called "interest." The amount of interest you must pay is added to the portion of the loan you must pay each month. In the long run, you'll end up paying more than the original price for the item you've purchased. BUT, in the short term, you can start using your purchase as soon as you buy it "on credit." Making an expensive purchase on credit is one of the features of having a bank account. It's very important to budget those monthly payments! If possible, pay back the loan as quickly as you can and that will lower the amount of interest you pay.

How Do I Get Started?

The first thing you must do is build credit, which essentially means proving that you can be trust to pay your bills

Quick Tips

- Every year federal law allows you access to one free credit report from annualcreditreport.com — take advantage of it.

- Your credit score is one of the most important things in your life from a financial perspective. A low credit score —under 600 — would mean that you would be denied for loans, or would have to pay the highest interest rates on any loaned money, including credit cards. The higher the better.

- Missing or making late payments can be disastrous to your credit score.

- It's better to pay off your card every month because your score is based on how responsible you are in using your credit.

on time. Every time you pay promptly, you earn points toward your overall "credit score." The higher your score, the more you'll be trusted by a lending organization, such as a bank, a car dealership, or a real estate agency. A lending organization will look at your credit score and analyze how likely you are to pay their loan back on time. Credit cards are a great way to build credit because you're expected to pay your credit card bill every month, like clockwork. Good credit means you have a good payment history. And that means you have an excellent credit score and are a great candidate for loans in the future.

However, if you accumulate lots of debt on your credit card and never pay them back on time, those cards can become your worst nightmare.

The Dangers of Credit Card Debt and How to Avoid It

What happens if you don't or can't pay your monthly credit card bill—or at least not all of it? The lending organization, let's say a bank, will automatically add a finance charge and interest on your monthly statement. These fees not only increase the amount of your monthly payment, but they also lower your credit score. Let's explore this more closely.

Credit cards make life a lot easier than carrying cash around. But, when you run out of cash, you stop spending. Credit cards don't run out ... and so, people tend to spend more money than they realize. At the end of the month when the credit card statement arrives, they are often shocked by the amount they've spent. Often, they can't pay off the entire bill. But that's okay, right? They can wait to pay the bill next month when they have more money in the bank. We already know the problem with that—a damaged credit score and hefty fees!

Interest is money that is paid to a lending organization at a certain rate based on the amount borrowed. When you get a credit card, an annual percentage rate will be applied to any late payments. These interest rates can range anywhere from 7% to 25% or more! Imagine that you build up a $1000 credit card bill over a year's time, and you have a 20% annual percentage rate. You'll owe $1200. That's $200 in interest because you didn't pay on time—$200 you could have had in your bank account for a future purchase. If you're not careful, credit card debt can accumulate quickly.

Personal Finance Stories

Kelly was able to get a credit card with a credit limit of $500 after she got her first job at the age of 17. Over the next few years, due to the fact that she was responsible with her spending and paid her bills on time, the credit card company rewarded her with credit increases. Soon, her credit limit was $2,000, and her credit score was 799.

However, after starting college, she had to start using her credit card for school supplies, books and meals. She also worked less, due to her full-time load of classes and before she knew it, she'd maxed out her credit card. To make matters worse, she applied for a few more credit cards and quickly maxed those out as well. She now owes about $10,000, and her monthly payments are around $350 per month, which she can't afford. Because she applied for so many cards, and has made a few late payments, her credit score has dropped to 643.

After speaking to her parents about the situation, they agreed to loan her the money to pay off her cards, but she'd have to lock up her cards and pay them back. On top of that, she's now using a credit monitoring app on her phone that gives her tips on how to improve her credit. And, once her parents paid the cards off, her credit score jumped back up to 725.

You can avoid credit card debt by building wise budgeting habits. First, don't spend money you know you won't have. If your monthly budget is $500, it would not be wise to spend $700 on your credit card. When you use your credit card, pretend that you're spending the money right then and there. Keep your receipts and add them up every time you make a purchase so you always know what you've spend. You also might want to set up automatic payments for your cell phone service, car loan or other monthly expenses. This way you'll never forget to pay these recurring bills.

Always do your research. Make sure the credit card you apply for will benefit your exact needs. If you drive a lot, get a credit card that earns gas points. See if you can find a card that doesn't have an annual fee. And definitely avoid getting a card because it has lots of fun rewards. That's exactly how you end up overspending and in debt. Research is the most important step in each phase of your path to financial independence. If you know exactly what you need and how to get it, your life will be much easier.

There are other ways to build your credit than using a credit card. You can apply for a credit-builder loan (which works like a credit card, but is solely used to build your credit); you can pay your monthly bills on time; and you can talk to your parents about creative options. The goal is what matters: earning a good credit score by developing good financial habits!

Exercise: Reading a Credit Card Statement

Know What You Spent

Every month you will receive a credit card statement in the mail or online. It will give you a minimum payment amount and the due date, the total amount you owe, the credit you have left, and a list of each item you purchased that month.

Exercise: Reading Your Credit Statement

Let's answer a few questions about the statement shown to the right:

1. How much total credit does he have (credit line)?
2. How much credit is available to spend?
3. What is the balance (how much he owes)?
4. When is the minimum payment due?
5. How much is the minimum payment? Should he only pay the minimum or more?
6. What is the Annual Percentage Rate for purchases?
7. How much did he pay last month?

CREDIT CARD STATEMENT			SEND PAYMENT TO Box 1244 Anytown, USA	
ACCOUNT NUMBER 4125-239-412	NAME John Doe	STATEMENT DATE 2/13/09	PAYMENT DUE DATE 3/09/09	
CREDIT LINE $1200.00	CREDIT AVAILABLE $1074.76	NEW BALANCE $125.24	MINIMUM PAYMENT DUE $20.00	

REFERENCE	SOLD	POSTED	ACTIVITY SINCE LAST STATEMENT	AMOUNT
483GE7382		1/25	PAYMENT THANK YOU	-168.80
32F349ER3	1/12	1/15	RECORD RECYCLER ANYTOWN, USA	14.83
89102DIS2	1/13	1/15	BEEFORAMA REST ANYTOWN, USA	30.55
NX34FJD32	1/18	1/18	GREAT ESCAPES BIG CITY, USA	27.50
84RT3293A	1/20	1/21	DINO-GEL GASOLINE ANYTOWN, USA	12.26
973DWS321	2/09	2/09	SHIRTS 'N SUCH TINYVILLE, USA	40.10

Previous Balance	(+)	168.80	Current Amount Due	125.24
Purchases	(+)	125.24	Amount Past Due	
Cash Advances	(+)		Amount Over Credit Line	
Payments	(-)	168.80	Minimum Payment Due	20.00
Credits	(-)			
FINANCE CHARGES	(+)			
Late Charges	(+)			
NEW BALANCE	(=)	125.24		

FINANCE CHARGE SUMMARY	PURCHASES	ADVANCES	For Customer Service Call: 1-800-xxx-xxxx For Lost or Stolen Card, Call: 1-800-xxx-xxxx 24-Hour Telephone Numbers
Periodic Rate	1.65%	0.54%	
Annual Percentage Rate	19.80%	6.48%	

The Importance of Saving

Why Do I Need To Know This?

Saving money for the future, for a big purchase or for an emergency, is just as important as putting money in your checking account to pay for your daily expenses. Let's say you want to buy a car and you plan on financing the car with a car loan. You have checked your budget and you can afford the monthly payments and still maintain your good credit. In order to get the car loan, you'll need to make a "down payment", which is money you must give to the loan company to get your loan started. The down payment lets you have the car—let's you drive it home! The amount of a down payment might be $1,000, $2,000 or even $5,000, depending on the sales price of the car and on your credit score. Most people save that sum of money up in their savings account over a period of time. They also earn a small amount of interest on their savings, which means their money grows just by sitting in the bank.

How Do I Get Started?

You already have a basic bank account, a good sense of your monthly budget and a credit card. Now, let's look at a savings account, which is a type of bank account that helps you save money, usually for emergencies. Savings are very helpful if you lose your job, have unexpected expenses, or need extra money (more than you have in your regular bank account) right away. You never know when you'll need it; when you do, you'll be grateful you have it.

Most banks can offer interest rates for savings accounts. This means that a small percentage of money, often less

Quick Tips

- Setting up automatic transfers from your checking account to your savings account is the simplest way to start saving.

- Automatically deposit a percentage of each paycheck into an account. Once it's set up, you won't even notice that the money is coming out of your check. Before you know it, you'll have a pile of cash ready for a rainy day.

- Apps, like Acorns, help you round-up your purchases to the nearest dollar and deposit it into your savings account. It's super easy and you can monitor it from your mobile device.

than 1%, will be added to your savings account every year. Every bank offers different interest rates, so be sure to do your research!

If you start saving early in your life, you will accumulate a lot of money over time. It is really important to have an account like this. Even if you don't earn interest on this account, make it a habit to add money to it regularly. For instance, you can set up automatic transfers from your checking to your savings account on a daily, weekly, monthly or even yearly basis. If you transfer $20 per month, that's $240 a year. If you have a savings account for 20 years, that turns into $4800! Whatever amount you can spare each month is worth transferring to your savings. Then, when you have an unexpected or extra large expense, you won't have to worry because you'll have the funds to cover it.

Other Ways To Save

We've talked a lot about savings accounts, but there are other kinds of accounts that are also great ways to save money—sometimes tax-free. After you've been budgeting, spending, and saving for awhile, you'll be ready to dive into the pool of alternate savings devices. And don't forget—always start by researching the options!

Individual Retirement Accounts (IRAs) are a type of savings account that help you save for retirement and offers some tax advantages. There are two types, include a Traditional IRA and a Roth IRA. Roth's can be a good option for younger people who aren't making a lot of money.

401(k) accounts are employer retirement plan accounts. Everyone should participate in this option, especially if your employer provides a match—meaning for every dollar you put in, your employer contributes a certain amount, too. That's free money! Your goal should be to contribute at least the maximum amount your employer will match. The earlier you start saving for retirement, the better off you'll be when you get there—we're talking multi-millionaire status.

Personal Finance Stories

Jake wants to save money but tends to live paycheck to paycheck and has a hard time finding a way to transfer money into his savings account every week or even each month. So, after doing some research online, he found an app that enables him to connect his bank accounts and credit cards to the app. Then, every time he makes a purchase using those linked cards or accounts, the purchase is rounded up to the nearest dollar, and the change is added to a savings account in the app. For example, if he buys a coffee drink for $2.45, the app rounds it up to $3 and the extra $0.55 is added to the app. It's basically a "set it and forget it strategy" for saving.

Jake has been using the app for over a year now and has been able to save more than $1,000, just with roundups of his "pocket change." He barely misses the extra change is able to save, and is excited to see his savings growing. His new goal is to save more quickly, so he's changed a setting in the app too add $10 per week on top of the roundups. Jake has discovered that saving money is actually fun!

Exercise: compounding interest

The More You Save, The More You Earn

When you open a checking account, often you can add a savings account at the same time. A savings account allows you to save money in the bank and earn money, called interest, based on the amount you're saving. The money you earn is called interest and how often you earn it depends on what type of savings account you have. Basiclly, interest is "free" money the bank pays you to keep in one of their accounts. The longer your money stays in the bank, the more money you earn.

Consider this example: would you rather have $10,000 right now, or a penny? You'd probably choose $10,000. But, what if I told you that the penny will double its value every day that you leave it in the bank? Now what would you choose? $10,000 now or the penny later? After 30 days, that penny would be worth $5.3 million, and by day 31, you'd have $10.7 million.

This is an exaggerated example, but it shows how compound interest works. Just a little bit of money left in an account over a longer period of time could grow substantially.

COMPOUNDING CALCULATOR	
DAY 1	$0.01
DAY 2	$0.02
DAY 3	$0.04
DAY 4	$0.08
DAY 5	$0.16
DAY 6	$0.32
DAY 7	$0.64
DAY 8	$1.28
DAY 9	$2.56
DAY 10	$5.12
DAY 11	$10.24
DAY 12	$20.48
DAY 13	$40.96
DAY 14	$81.92
DAY 15	$163.84
DAY 16	$327.68
DAY 17	$655.36
DAY 18	$1,310.72
DAY 19	$2,621.44
DAY 20	$5,242.88
DAY 21	$10,485.76
DAY 22	$20,971.52
DAY 23	$41,943.04
DAY 24	$83,886.08
DAY 25	$167,772.16
DAY 26	$335,544.32
DAY 27	$671,088.64
DAY 28	$1,342.177.28
DAY 29	$2,684,354.56
DAY 30	$5,368,709.12
DAY 31	$10,737.418.23

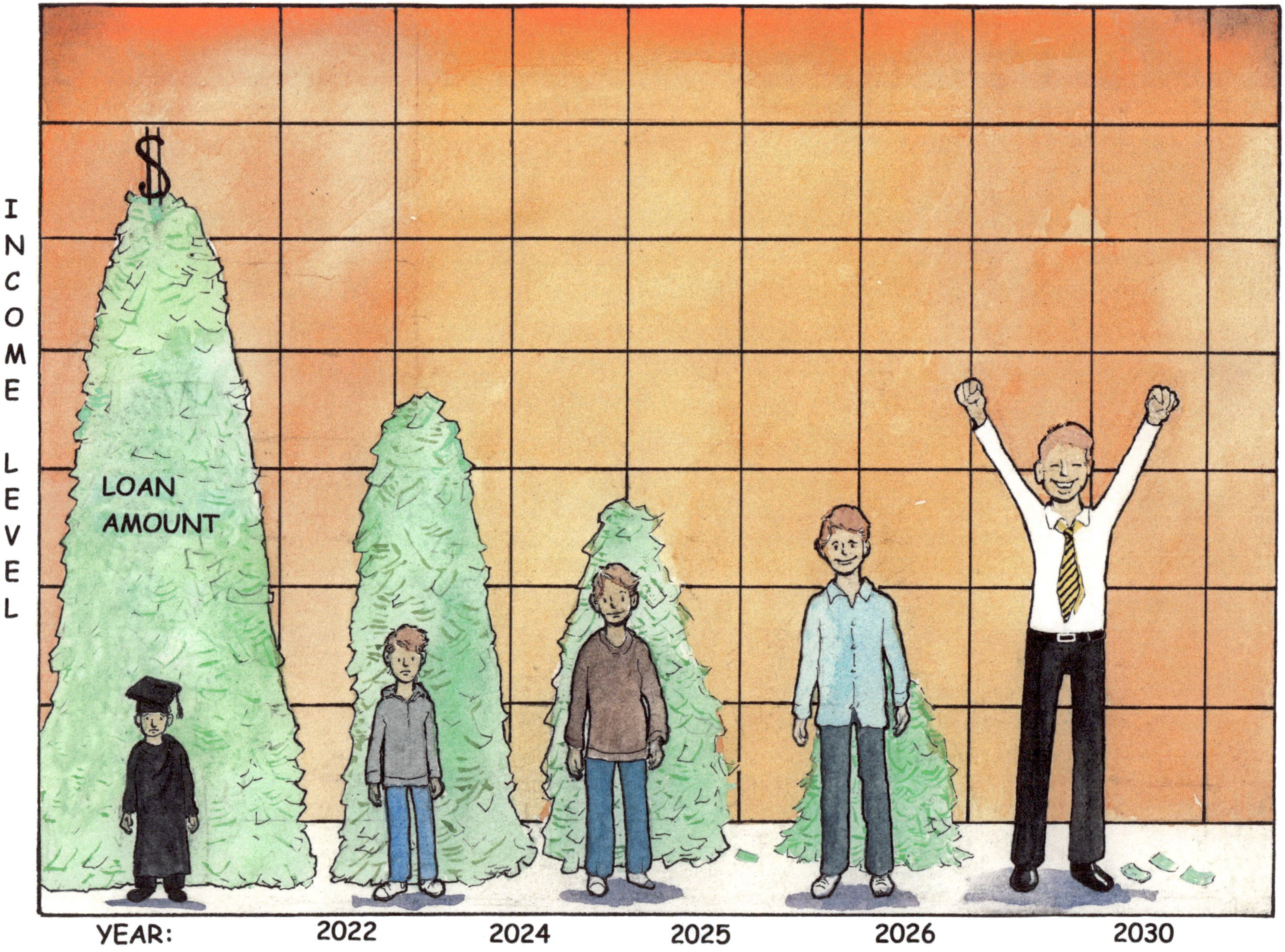
INCOME LEVEL
$
LOAN AMOUNT
YEAR:
2022
2024
2025
2026
2030

Using student loans

Why Do I Need To Know This?

A loan buys you time so that you can afford more education after high school. Maybe you want to go to college. Maybe you'd prefer to learn a technical trade. Maybe you want to take coding classes or train to become a commercial pilot. Whatever your interests are, it's likely that you'll need to earn a degree or complete a certification program after graduating from high school. And higher education can be really expensive. While some parents are able to help their kids with these expenses, many students must borrow money. That's what student loans are for. Why go into debt for more education? Because the more education you have, the more options you have for an interesting job and the more earning potential you have. The reality check is the whopper-sized loan you might have to pay back—$50,000—$100,000—$150,000! And you might have to start paying it back (only it small amounts!) before you find a good paying job. So, how do you deal with this big loan?

How Do I Get Started?

The years after high school graduation are an incredible time in your life. Going to college can make them even better. You're likely to live away from home and to make decisions for yourself for the first time. It's exciting! But it's also important to understand the obligations that come with borrowing money. Student loans can be your best friend, funding you all through college and then graduate school, if you choose to go. Loans can help you land and awesome job and set you on an exciting career path. But if you put off paying back the loans and accumulate thousands of dollars

Quick Tips

- Use an online calculator to figure out how long it will take to pay off your student loan, based on how much you'll be paying each month. You might surprised to see that an extra $50 per month, could save you a few months' worth of payments.

- Use a budgeting tool to add the expense to your monthly budget.

- Don't miss a payment or make any late payments—it can ruin your credit score. If you get into a bind and think you'll miss a payment, call the loan company to ask them to work with you.

- If interest rates drop, you should try to refinance to pay less interest.

in debt, loans can be your worst enemy. Listen to this: As of 2018, Americans owe $1.3 trillion in student loans and debt—yes, trillion! You don't want to become part of that horrifying statistic! But you can be smart about your student loans so that they don't backfire—and this is where we get started.

How do you pay off student loans?

First, find out how much you owe. Then set up a pay-off plan you can stick to. There will be a variety of payment plans you can choose from, so you'll want to research which one is best for you. Once you figure out how much you owe, start paying it off right away if you can. Many student loans have an initial grace period—a certain amount of time before you have to begin paying back the loan. Ignore the grace period, if you can, and start making payments! If you have a job, you should be able to pay off a couple hundred dollars a month. Even if $100 a month seems like a lot, it's worth the sacrifice to keep lowering the total amount you owe. You'll be done months, maybe even years, earlier than you expected.

Budgeting will be your new best friend when it comes to student loans—or any loans you might take out in the future. Add the "student loans" category to your budget. This is an expense you cannot ignore! So, you may have to cut down on luxury items such as eating out or concert tickets. The best advice that has helped people pay back their student loans is this: Maintain a simple lifestyle.

Be sure to cover all your expenses before you spend money on fun activities. If you receive any extra money, like a bonus or a gift, as tempting as it is to spend it frivolously, stop and think: why not use a portion of it to make an extra loan payment? Yes, you have graduated from college and you're earning a salary—you're in charge of your money. But that means you're responsible for your bills and should be wise about your spending habits.

Finally don't stress out. It might seem like it's going to take forever to pay that amount of money off, but once you land a good-paying job, your bigger paycheck should enable you to make larger payments. And every year you work, you'll get raises and bonuses, and eventually you'll leave that job and get a new one that pays you even more. The student loan gave you a leg up in the world, setting you up for a strong career path. One day, it will be paid off!

Personal Finance Stories

Matt's family isn't rich. His parents went to college and it was expected that he would too, but the thought of how to pay for it was stressful for the whole family. Matt got good grades and qualified for a small sports scholarship that paid for his first college semester, but the remaining semesters would have to come out of his pocket. So, he applied for a student loan through the university.

When he finished college, the total amount of his student loans was about $70,000. He had a grace period before he had to pay off the loans, but he decided to start paying $100 a month right away. After about six months, he was able to get an entry-level job in his field, earning him $60,000 per year. Because he lived with his parents, this income enabled him to pay about $500 a month toward his student loans. He added this amount to his budget, along with entertainment, car expenses, clothes, and the small amount of rent he paid to his parents for food and lodging. Also, anytime he got any extra money he'd put it toward the student loans.

Fast forward six years, when Matt was able to make his final payment for his student loans. What a relief!

Types of Student Loans

William D Ford Federal Direct Loan – Largest federal student loan program, made up of three different loan types:

1. **Direct Subsidized loans:** Designed for undergraduate students with financial needs, you can borrow up a certain amount each year to pay for school. Unlike other loans in this program, you're not charged interest on this loan while you're in school.
2. **Direct Unsubsidized loans:** Can be used by undergraduate, graduate and professional degree students. There is a limit on the amount borrowed each year. Unlike other loans, interest accrues on these loans while you're in school.
3. **Direct PLUS loans:** Designed for parents of under graduate students paying for their child's education or for graduate or professional degree students paying for their own education.

Subject	Federal Student Loan	Private Student Loan
Interest Rates	Rates are fixed and often lower than private loans.	Can have variable and fixed interest rates.
Subsidies	If you have financial need, you may qualify for a loan in which that government pays the interest while you are in school (subsidized loans).	Often not subsidized, you will be responsible for all of the interest on the loan.
Credit Check	You don't need to get a credit check to qualify for federal student loans.	Often requires an established credit record or co-signer.
Postponement Options	If you are having trouble repaying your loan, you may be able to temporarily postpone or lower your payments.	Often no options are given but still should check from your lender.
Loan Forgiveness	You maybe eligible to have some portion of your loans forgiven if you work in public service.	Often lenders do not offer loan forgiveness but some student loans from state agencies can be forgiven under certain circumstances.

Exercise: Applying for Federal Student Aid (FAFSA)

Get Your Documents In Order

One of the first things most students do when they are accepted at a college is apply for student aid. Filling out the Free Application for Student Aid (FAFSA) is usually one of the first steps, but the form can be complicated if you don't have all of your documents in order. Let's go through the exercise of making sure you're ready to go.

Exercise: FAFSA Checklist

Let's answer a few questions about the statement shown to the right.

When you are ready, the best way to fill out the FAFSA application is to do it online. There are help sections, frequently asked questions and calculators to help you out. You can sign and submit your application instantly, and if you have to stop and come back later, you can save it for another time.

FAFSA Checklist

Before You Start:

[ ] You are eligible.
(You are a U.S. citizen; have a valid Social Security number; graduated from a high school, earned a GED, or passed an ATB test; enrolled/accepted at a school that participates in the federal student aid program; don't owe a refund for a federal grant or defaulted on federal student loans.)

[ ] It is not past the deadline, which is normally the end of June or early July.

You have your:

[ ] Social Security number.

[ ] Driver's license/ID card.

[ ] Latest W-2 forms, income records for both students and parents.

[ ] Student's most recent Federal Income Tax Returns.

[ ] Parent's most recent Federal Income Tax Returns.

[ ] Most recent untaxed income records.

[ ] Latest bank statements.

[ ] Records of income from investments and business ventures.

[ ] Alien registration number or permanent residence card if you are not a U.S. citizen.

Getting a Car Loan

Why Do I Need To Know This?

Buying a car is usually the first major purchase you will make. Saving for the down payment on a car is a whole lot easier and faster than saving the whole amount. Most people—young or old—just don't want to wait that long! Many adults can't afford to pay in full for a car or choose not to because they can put their money to better use by taking out a car loan. The point is, a car loan is something you're likely to encounter a few times in your life.

How Do I Get Started?

You can finally drive and you want your own car! You've waited for this moment since before you got your license! But cars are expensive, and you don't have the money to buy one. Your best option is a car loan.

A loan of any type starts with something you have already learned about—credit history. If you have been using a credit card responsibly, then you will have a great credit score, which makes you a good candidate for a car loan. If you don't yet have a credit history, you will need a parent or guardian's help to qualify for a loan. Your credit score affects the interest rate you receive on the loan. A high credit score earns you a lower interest rate on your loan, which means you'll pay less for the car overall.

The next step is also something you know about: budgeting. Figure out how much you can afford to pay each month for your car loan. Add the category, "car loan," into your budget so you're sure to remember to save for it.

Quick Tips

- There are a lot of online calculators that can help you figure out how much car you can afford, based on the price, the interest rate, and insurance rates.

- As enticing as it is to get the fanciest car out there, be realistic with what you can afford. It's just a set of wheels to get you from point A to point B. Sports cars and luxury vehicles tend to have higher insurance rates, so factor in that cost as well.

- The higher the interest rate, the more you'll pay for the car. A low interest rate would be from 0-2%; anything over 10% would be considered high. Factor that into the cost.

Once you feel sure you can stick to your budget, it's time to get pre-approved for the loan. What does that mean? It means doing your research—just like you have in each step of your progress toward financial independence. You never want to skip this one!

Take a look at different financial institutions or online loan providers to see which company will provide you with the best loan option. It might be a loan that has a low interest rate but lasts five years—and you can't pay it off sooner. Or it could be a loan that has a higher interest rate but gives you flexibility when it comes to how quickly you can pay it off. Once you decide on the loan terms that work for you, you'll need to complete an application to see if you qualify for the loan. If you do, you'll receive a "pre-approval," which means you have permission to spend a certain amount of money for a certain amount of time. In other words, you are pre-approved and can now start car shopping. Now the fun begins! Just be sure the fun stays within your budget.

The bank will give you a "pre-approval" letter that you'll take with you to the car dealership. Treat that letter like cash! It's the golden ticket that basically says the bank will loan you the money to purchase a car. The dealer will then show you cars within your price range and you should be able to drive home the one you choose that same day.

Other Options

An alternative to getting a car loan through a bank is a loan through the dealership where you buy your car. Car dealerships have their own financing department and their loans are similar to bank loans. It's a good idea to bring an adult with you to help you understand the loan terms, ask the right questions and make sure you're getting a good interest rate and not overpaying for the car. Sometimes it's better to walk away and think about the decision before you make it.

Car loans are common. As long as you make your monthly payments on time and don't fall behind, you'll pay off the loan within five years and build your credit in the process. That's a good deal!

Personal Finance Stories

Becca was excited to buy her first car. She'd been driving her old family car through high school, which was fine (and free), but after getting her first real job, she felt like it was time to buy a "grown-up car." She knew she could comfortably afford about $250 per month and wanted to keep her car insurance affordable, so she decided to get a pre-owned car that was one or two years old.

Using her bank's mobile app, she filled out the used car loan application and was surprised to discover that within a few minutes she was pre-approved. The loan company emailed her the pre-approval letter the next day, and she and her dad headed to the dealership that weekend. They looked at a variety of cars until she found one she loved. The dealership had a "no haggle" price policy, which meant that she had to pay the sticker price - there was no room to negotiate. She handed the dealership her letter, signed a few documents, and drove off the lot that same day.

Becca has added the $250 cost to her monthly budget and uses her mobile app to make automatic payments.

Car Loan Tips

Tip 1: Shop the loan separately from the car

Before starting negotiations on the exact car and price, begin the loan application process with credit unions, banks, well-respected online lenders, or your auto insurance company. Our research indicates that online banks have been the best place to find a good loan, but credit unions are also competitive, and their rates tend to be about 1% to 1.5% lower than bank rates.

Tip 2: Credit Score

"Credit" is a very important concept to understand. It can make a big difference to your lifestyle and the choices you qualify to make. Good credit means good options, which usually means a better lifestyle. If you have a job, it is not difficult to establish a solid credit history. Many young adults who are buying their first car choose a "student loan," which has a much higher interest rate than a conventional loan. If you're a recent graduate or a college student with a good credit history, some car dealers offer special incentives to get you to buy a car. For instance, you might qualify for a discount because you've graduated frorm high school or college less than two years ago. Whatever the sweet deal might be, make sure you can afford the car before you buy it!

Tip 3: Co-Signer

If you can cover the car payments and other vehicle costs but lenders won't approve you for loan, a co-signer should be a good solution. A co-signer can be a family member, or a relative or a close friend. However, only use a co-signer when you're sure you can cover the loan payments. If not, the lender will go after the co-signer to pay, and their credit score will sink!

2016 Toyota Camry
$23,000
66 Month Term

Person A	Person B
Credit Score: 730	Credit Score: 599
Interest Rate: 1.99%	Interest Rate: 14.99%
Payment: $368.22	Payment: $513.97
Total Interest Paid: $1,302.39	Total Interest Paid: $10,921.44
Total of Payments: $24,302.39	Total of Payments: $33,921.44

Person B pays

$9,619.05 MORE

than Person A for the exact same vehicle and the exact same sticker price

The example shown above illustrates the importance of having a good credit score, which qualifies you for a better, lower interest rate. A lower interest rate will lower your monthly payment, enabling you to pay less interest over the life of the loan and making your overall purchase price much lower as well.

If you already have a good credit score, look into different lenders to make sure you are getting the lowest rate possible. Every point lowers your monthly payment.

Exercise: Car Loan Calculator

Champagne Wishes and Caviar Dreams

That's a quote from an old television show about the rich and famous. When you consider purchasing your first car, it's easy to start dreaming of a luxury car with all the bells and whistles. However, being realistic with your budget is always the better option. It's not just the price of the car; it's also the other costs that come into play when it comes to maintaining the vehicle. For instance, luxury cars often require a more expensive blend of gasoline, have higher maintenance costs, and higher insurance premiums. Choosing a more affordable vehicle will fit within yoour budget and can still turn heads.

To Buy or To Lease - That is the Question

Purchasing a car means that you will own the car outright once you've paid it off. You'll take out a loan, make payments for a specific amount of time, and after your last payment, you'll receive the title and registration in your name. You will own the car free and clear (other than maintenance) until you sell or donate it. Leasing a car is similar in that you'll make monthly payments for the car, but it will continue to be owned by the dealership until your payment term ends. And then you will be given the option to give the car back to the dealer and choose another car (starting a new payment contract), or purchase the car (starting a purchase agreement). Leases can allow you to drive a more expensive car for a lower monthly payment, but there are restrictions on how many miles you can drive the car per year, and you are required to rigorously maintain the vehicle so that the dealer can resell it once your lease term is over.

Exercise: Using A Car Loan Calculator

The easiest way to figure out how much you can afford to spend on a car is to go to your internet browser and search for "Car Loan Calculator". You'll be asked how much money you plan to put down, how much your loan will be for (car cost minus your down payment), the interest rate (depending on your lender), and the loan period (the number of months you'll be paying the loan back). With that information, you can usually find out what your monthly payment will look like. Be smart and don't get in over your head.

The Basics of doing taxes

Why Do I Need To Know This?

First of all, what are taxes? How do they work? Why do we have to do them? Here's what you need to know before we dive into how to do them.

Taxes are fees that are taken out of individual's or corporation's paycheck in order to pay for government activities. It helps fund government activities that, hopefully, will help benefit society. Why do we have to pay taxes? It's the law.

There are many kinds of taxes—corporate, sale, property, estate, and more. But the most common kind, the one that relates specifically to working professionals, is income tax.

Income tax is a percentage of individual earnings that's paid to the federal government. The amount of taxes you pay depends on the amount you earn, and the amount you earn determines which tax bracket you're in. Each bracket includes a specific earnings range. The more money you make, the higher your tax bracket—and the more taxes you'll pay. Taxes are automatically taken out of your paycheck, so there's nothing more you need to do until early Spring.

What does "file taxes" mean? Well, every Spring, people submit tax returns to the Internal Revenue Service, the IRS. The deadline to file a return is usually April 15th. If you've ever seen adults scrambling the first two weeks of April with receipts and endless paperwork, it's probably because they're preparing their taxes. If you have paid too

Quick Tips

- When you are young, doing your taxes can take as little as 10-15 minutes. Just make sure you've got your documents ready.

- When you get a job, they'll have you fill out a W-4 form, which is where you tell them about your exemptions. All that means is how much tax should be taken out of your paycheck. For young adults that are single, it's usually a 0 or 1. Zero means that the maximum amount of taxes will be taken out, that you'll likely get a refund, but it's also like loaning the government money until refund time comes. Talk to your parents about your best options. The goal is not to owe any money at tax time.

much tax over the course of the previous year, you will receive a tax refund. If you haven't paid enough tax throughout the year, you will need to send a tax payment with your tax return. Taxes can be complex, which is why many adults pay an accountant to help them prepare their returns. This is why understanding the basics of how to file is so important.

How Do I Get Started?

To begin, you need a few required documents. The first one is called a W-2 form. You'll receive it in the mail from your employer, usually between mid-January to early February. It reports your annual wages earned and the taxes that have been withheld. A W-2 will be sent to you every year you work, for the rest of your career. You'll receive two copies—one to send in your tax return and one to keep with a copy of your tax return. It's important to keep a copy of your tax returns for at least ten years. The next important documents you need are: a form of identification (like a passport or license), residency status (a passport works), your social security number, a copy of your last tax return, a bank statement showing any interest your bank account(s) earned, proof of any tax credits, deductions or exclusions (you probably won't have to worry about this), and your bank account information. Finally, if you're going to college, you'll probably get a form from your school that provides information about college expenses, books, tuition.

Once you have these documents in hand, you're ready to fill out a 1040 tax form. You can usually get the form from your local library or post office. You can also use an online tax service, like TurboTax, which walks you through each step of filling out the form. There are plenty of online resources to answer any question you have or you can contact the IRS through its website.

Budgeting and knowing where your documents are (store them safely in a folder or envelope!) make tax time painless. Many apps for managing your money will also allow you to export your data directly into your online tax program. Filing your tax return is not as complicated as you think, especially if you're single and have no dependents.

Personal Finance Stories

Tina got her first job last year at the local mall, while still going to school. She works as a barista at the local coffee shop, gets paid fairly well, earns tips from customers, and has a flexible schedule that works around her classes. It's the beginning of the new year, and she's starting to think about filing her tax return. Her job sent her a W-2 detailing her annual wages and taxes paid, her school sent her a 1098-T detailing her school expenses, and she's been pretty good about keeping track of her tips.

Tina decided to use an online tax preparation software, which is free for someone in her income bracket with an incomplicated tax return. She entered her personal information, her bank account information (for a potential refund), her W2 was able to import directly into the program, she manually copied the information from her 1098-T, and then she answered a few other questions about her job, tips, life, automobile registration, etc.

Within 15 minutes, Tina was done and was excited to find out that she'd be getting about $1,000 back in federal and state refunds — money she's planning to use for a mini-vacation. Now all she had to do is wait for the refund to be automatically deposited into her bank account by the IRS.

Tax Terms 101

1. **Earned Income** – salaries, wages, tips, professional fees, including taxable scholarships
2. **Unearned Income** – investment-type income like interest on your savings account, dividends on capital gains, unemployment compensation.
3. **Gross Income** – all income you received in the form of money, goods, property and services that are not exempted from tax.
4. **Exemptions** – a monetary amount that you can deduct from your taxable income for basic living expenses. Dependent children (which you are to your parents) qualify as exemptions.
5. **Standard Deduction** – a monetary amount the federal government gives you if you meet certain criteria (differs according to marital status).
6. **Itemized Deduction** – Reduces the amount of tax you owe to the government. Categories of expenses that can be deducted are: medical & dental, taxes, interest, charitable contributions, & casualty and theft losses.
7. **W-2 Forms** – Wage-income form that an employee receives from the employer in order to prepare individual tax returns.
8. **Filing Status** – whether you are single, married or, head of household (there are several sub-categories within those).

As a student your income will probably not reach filing minimums, but you're still having taxes taken out by the federal government. If you file, you're likely to get that money back. If you choose not to file, then the government will gladly keep your money!

Types of Forms:
- **1040EZ** - one page, simplest tax form requires a taxable income of less than $50,000.
- **1040A** – a complicated form that allows flexibility in sources of income, cannot itemize deductions but can deduct IRA contributions.
- **1040** – "long" form, the most complicated form; required if income is above $50,000. Itemizes deductions to adjust income.

DEADLINE for taxes is April 15th. You can get an automatic four-month extension to "file," but you still have to pay taxes by April 15th.

Exercise: Tax Rates

Nothing Is Certain But Death and Taxes

Using the tax rate table shown below, we can figure out the effective tax rate for a specific income level. In our example, our employee makes $200,000 in annual taxable income. In the table to the left, you can see how your entire $200,000 income would not be taxed at 9.55% - only the amount above $46,767. The income is instead broken up into six segments and each segment is taxed separately. The solution to the right, shows how the income would be taxed. You can also figure out the effective tax rate by taking $16,809.77 and dividing by the income of $200,000, giving you an effective tax rate of 8.4%.

Taxable Income	Marginal Tax Rate
$0 - $7,124	1.25%
$7,125 - $16,890	2.25%
$16,891 - $26,657	4.25%
$26,658 - $37,005	6.25%
$37,006 - $46,766	8.25%
$46,767 - $1,000,000	9.55%
$1,000,001 +	10.55%

Taxable Income	Marginal Tax Rate	Tax
$7,124	1.25%	$89.05
$9,766	2.25%	$219.74
$9,767	4.25%	$415.10
$10,348	6.25%	$646.75
$9,761	8.25%	$805.28
$153,234	9.55%	$14,633.85
$200,000		**$16,809.77**

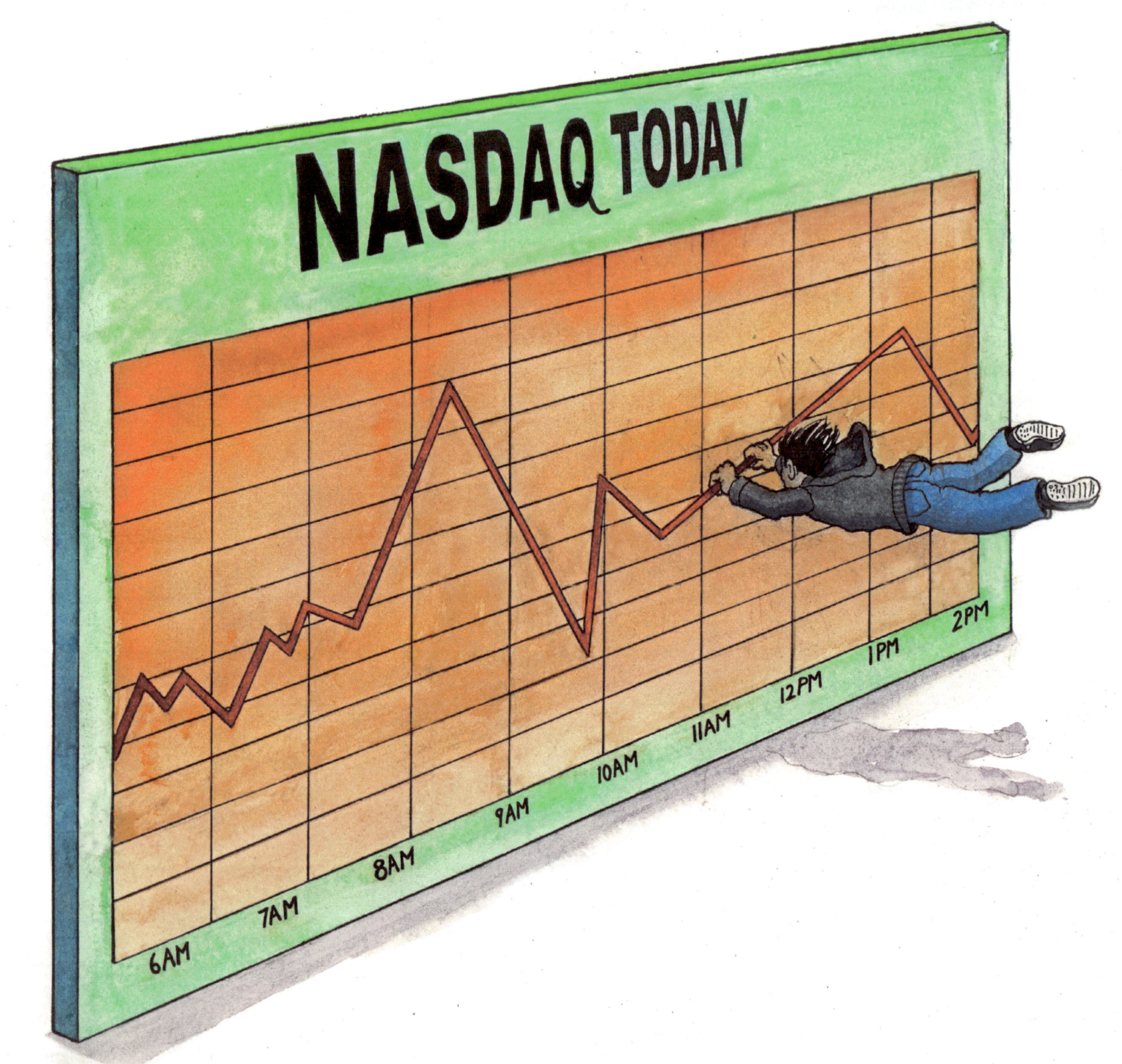

Stock Market Basics

Why Do I Need To Know This?

People who want financial independence learn quickly that the best way to achieve it is to make their money work for them. They don't just store it in a bank account. They invest it with the hope that their investment rises in value over a period of time. When they're ready to sell their investment, they expect to have made a good amount of money. The stock market is one way to put your money to work for your future benefit. Money in your savings account will earn an average of 2% interest. That amount does not add up quickly! Money invested in the stock market has the potential to earn a lot more—5%, 8%, 10% maybe. It also has the potential to lose you money if the investment loses value. In other words, investing in the stock market is risky.

For that reason, the stock market isn't for everyone. It takes—you guessed it—research to understand how stocks (and bonds) work, to invest wisely, and to have the courage to make rational decisions instead of emotional ones. The point is, understanding how the stock market works will help you make more educated decisions when the time comes for you to start saving for your retirement. And a retirement fund is an important part of being financially independent. Mutual funds are a portfolio of stocks managed by a company with the goal of making money for a small fee. At some point, you will have the option to invest in a retirement plan, often called a 401(k) or a 403(b), offered by your employer. When we talked about a savings account, we mentioned investing a small amount of money into mutual funds that should increase in value over a long period of time, creating your retirement fund.

Quick Tips

- There are lots of apps to help you learn how to invest in the stock market. Just make sure you are aware of the fees that get charged per trade. Search for "investing for free" and you should find some good options.

- We can't state this enough: past performance does not guarantee future results. Just because a stock has done well in the past, doesn't mean it wo;; continue to do well — you could lose all of your money. Be sure you understand the risks before you invest this way.

- Short-term investing isn't usually a good plan. Investing is something you do for the long term.

How Do I Get Started?

The stock market is where people buy and sell shares of stocks. When you buy a stock, you own a share (a small piece) of a public company. The stock represents a portion of a company's assets and earnings. The better a company is doing, the more the stock is worth.

The stock market has been around since 1792—it's been an integral part of our financial society. After all that time, there are still no tricks or shortcuts to investing and making money instead of losing it. As a result, a LOT of people have made AND lost money in the stock market. Even so, it continues to be one of the best ways to make your money work for you.

Two well-known stock market exchanges—where investments, or "share," are bought and sold—are the New York Stock Exchange and the Nasdaq. The NYSE is on Wall Street in New York City. The Nasdaq is online.

The stock market works like an auction. You want to buy low and sell high. That's how you make money. Say you buy stock "XYZ" for $5 a share. Then company XYZ develops a new product, and it takes off. People are buying up the product and they're excited about company XYZ. The value of your stock increases to $30 a share. The value of your stock increases to $30 a share. You decide that's a pretty good return on your investment, so you sell your shares on the stock market. The person who buys your shares imagines that company XYZ is going to continue to do well. Meanwhile, you just made a profit of $25! It may be that the new owner also makes a profit if the stock continues to grow. And then you might feel disappointed that you sold so quickly. BUT, at any moment, company XYZ could experience a huge production problem or scandal that causes the stock to drop sharply. Now that stock is down to $1. A lot of money could be lost this way.

Trying to predict when companies will be doing well and when they will do poorly is the game called "playing the stock market." And it's not easy! You want to make predictions on when you think companies will be on the rise

Personal Finance Stories

Matt signed up for an online stock investing fund through his mobile device. He has a little bit of money tucked away in a savings account and decided to play the stock market to see if he could make a bit more money faster. The app doesn't charge any fees, so he can trade as much as he wants to.

He got a tip about this hot new stock where he could potentially triple his money. It's risky, but he decided to invest $500 in the stock and see how it goes. The first week the stock skyrocketed and he made about $50, so he let it ride hoping to triple his money. The second week, the stock was still doing well and he made another $50, so he continued to let it ride. Over the next few weeks, he continued to watch the stock go up, until one day, there was some bad news about the company and the stock tanked 50%. Ouch. His $500 investment had gone up over $600, but with this news, was now worth about $300. Worried, he sold all of the stock and swallowed hard over his $200 loss.

The stock market is full of risks, along with normal ups and downs. Think about longer-term stocks and companies that you trust and even use their products. Most of all, understand that you could lose all of your money at any time.

Exercise: Stock Diversification

Don't Put All Your Eggs In One Basket

The old saying, "Don't put all of your eggs in one basket" simply means that if you drop the basket, you'll break all of your eggs and have nothing left. The same concept goes for buying stocks and it's called stock diversification. Simply put, it means that buying five stocks is better than buying one stock. And, buying stocks in different industries is typically less risky than buying just one kind of stock, such as all technology stocks.

Pro Tips:

- Invest in the business you understand
- Don't try to time the Market
- Do not let emotions cloud your judgment
- Create a broad portfolio
- Have a realistic expectation and be patient
- Invest for the long term and monitor regularly

Exercise: Finding Profit

Find out the profit made in the following cases:

- **Budget:** $2,000
- **Stock Purchased:** Apple (AAPL)
- **Market Price:** $162
- **Dealer Brokerage Fee:** $5 per trade

Amount invested:

(Number of shares purchased) x (Price per share) + Dealer Brokerage Fee = $_____

Amount Sold For: (Assume stock rose by 8%)

(Number of shares invested) x (Price per share) + Dealer Brokerage Fee = $_____

Profit:

(Amount Sold For) - (Amount Invested) = $_____

Answer:
Profit: $145.52

and on the fall. One of the best strategies is to focus on long term investments. Rather than constantly trading your stocks, you can earn a higher return if you let the stock grow over time. Stocks will always experience daily ups and downs, so it takes a patient waiting of a number of years to earn the highest return.

Now that you have a basic idea of how the stock market works, how do you actually invest? Online. There are lots of websites and applications where you can invest. Some of the programs have trade fees while others are completely free. Do your research and find the best platform for you. There are thousands and thousands of resources online to help you learn how to invest wisely into the stock market. If you do well, you may become the next Warren Buffet! If you don't know who that is, look him up. Trust me. He is the stock market king.

Various kinds of insurance and how to get them

Why Do I Need To Know This?

If you ever decide to get a loan to buy a car, or eventually a home, the lender will require you to have insurance to protect their investment. Lenders don't want to lose money! Insurance gives you and the lender "peace of mind" because if an unexpected situation arises, like a car accident or a flood in the basement, insurance will cover most of the repair costs. Plus, in some states, it's the law to have insurance. The type of insurance and the amount of coverage you get are important decisions to make based on your best friend—research!

How Do I Get Started?

Throughout a person's life, a variety of different insurance products could be used. In many cases, insurance is a kind of protection in a sudden, unexpected, and costly situation that can happen to anyone at any time. Accidents and natural disasters are good examples. In some cases, insurance can also be a retirement asset or an estate-planning tool.

Types of Insurance Coverage:

Property insurance, auto (or other vehicle) insurance, health insurance, life insurance, and (depending on your net worth and assets you own) umbrella and indemnity insurance are available options that provide coverage for your most important assets. The most relevant to young adults are heath insurance and car insurance.

Quick Tips

- Car insurance is relatively simple to get and you can get discounts for good grades, having multiple cars, being a good driver ... even for having certain safety features on your car. Sometimes it's worth it to share insurance with your parents early on, just for the discounts.

- Medical insurance is usually provided as a benefit by your employer. But when you're a young adult, you'll often stay on your parents insurance until you're around the age of 25.

- You can switch insurance anytime in order to get the best rates, so make sure you check rates every year.

Health Insurance: Protecting your family with health insurance is essential. Health insurance covers medical and surgical expenses that you may incur. Medical bills are often high, and your policy may only cover part of the bill. Unforeseen medical costs can deplete your savings, especially if you are unable to work while you are sick or injured. It's important to have appropriate coverage.

Health insurance policies will either reimburse you for your expenses while sick or injured or pay the health care provider directly.

The amounts of coverage and the deductibles as well as your policy exclusions are personal preferences that seem to vary with the level of your family's net worth. The higher your net worth, the higher your coverage limits. Be sure you understand the limits of your health insurance policy.

Many people receive health insurance from the company where they work. Often it's part of the employee benefits package, and the quality of the coverage can cause a potential employee to accept or reject a job offer.

Auto Insurance: Vehicle policies cover the costs associated with getting into a car accident and often include liability coverage, which would cover the cost of the damage you cause another vehicle. Other options include comprehensive, medical and car rental coverage. Most states require all vehicle owners to purchase a minimum amount of auto insurance, but many people choose to purchase additional insurance to give them further coverage. Premiums will vary based on age, gender, years of driving experience, accident and moving violation history, along with a variety of other factors.

Personal Finance Stories

When Billy bought his first car, he financed it through the dealership. Before he could drive it off the lot, he had to provide proof of automobile insurance. Using his mobile device, he was able to get a few quotes and instantly signed up for the insurance he needed.

As it turned out, it was a good thing the lender required insurance because later that year, Billy was in a car accident. It wasn't his fault but his insurance carrier was able to negotiate with the other person's insurance carrier and resolve the issue quickly. While his car was being fixed, Billy's insurance company gave him a rental car.

But that wasn't the end of it. When Billy's car was rear-ended, he hurt his back and knee, and was sent to the hospital to be checked out. After a few hours in the emergency room, and some pain medication, he was able to walk out.

The cost to fix the car was $5,000 and the cost for the ER visit was $12,000, all paid for through insurance. Without it, he would have had to try to convince the person who hit him to help with the costs, or he would have been on the hook for the full $17,000 himself.

Car Insurance Tips

Review Your Insurance Policy Every Couple of Months:

The competition among insurance companies fluctuates frequently due to ever-changing business demands/needs. Often when you get comfortable with your insurance company, it's important to keep tabs on insurance rates - they have a tendency to creep up while other companies are lowering their rates. They get away with it because so many customers don't notice!

Discounts:

Be sure to ask if there are any discounts available for your insurance policy. Most companies have discounts for being a good student, a non-smoker, a good driver, a graduate of an authorized driving school, a child of someone who has served in the miitary or working in the government. It never hurts to ask!

Comparison Sites:

There are many websites and online tools that will help you compare the prices and products offered by different auto insurance companies. Use them!

Driving Habits:

One of the best ways to get a good insurance rate is to improve your driving, which minimizes the possibiity of an accident (the goal of every insurance company!). Many insurance companies are using "telematic devices" that are installed in your vehicle to record driving habits. The information is sent to the company to help determine your insurance rate.

Exercise: Life Insurance

Living The Dream Starts With Making The Right Investments

We believe that life insurance is the bridge that gets you over life's bumps in the road, whether it's a job loss, an illness, or a death. Getting insurance early in life can make your annual premiums cheaper and finance college, a wedding, or a new house, depending on the type of policy you get. The important thing to know is that it's not all about dying - it's more about living.

There are two types of life insurance — term life and whole life.

Term Life: This provides protection for a specific, limited amount of time (like 10, 15, 20, 25 or 30 years, or up to a maximum age, like 80). Usually there is no cash value, but you'll pay a lower premium. It often offers protection for specific times of need, like a mortgage or a child's college tuition.

Whole Life: This is designed to stay inforce for an individual's entire life — normally until age 120. It has a cash value that accumulates over the life of the policy, meaning that you can access the cash for any reason, and it becomes guaranteed income after retirement. It's a great part of a complete financial plan.

Exercise: Life Insurance Calculator

Calculating life insurance is as easy as going online and inputting some numbers into one of the many life insurance calculators on the internet. Some of the things you should know ahead of time are that men have higher premiums than women, and smokers pay more than non-smokers. Many insurers will also ask for a physical exam by a doctor prior to providing insurance, to find out if there are any pre-existing conditions or family history. These are all the more reasons to explore life insurance when you're young and healthy.

Retirement Accounts

Why Do I Need To Know This?
Retirement. You're kidding, right? No kidding. If you want to be able to retire, you need to think about it a lot sooner than you might imagine. When we talked about savings, we introduced the idea of setting up a retirement account. We also talked briefly about retirement when we discussed the stock market. The more time you have to save, the more money you'll have to live on when you retire—when you stop earning a consistent and sizable salary. The fact is, by today's calculations, you're likely to need at least a million dollars to be able to live a modest life. Not a Starbucks life; more like a McDonald's life. That's why it's important to start thinking about retirement when you're young.

How Do I Get Started?
You know the answer—always begin with research! Ask your parents and your grandparents about their retirement plans. Go online to learn more, Retirement accounts include 401(k)s, Individual Retirement Accounts (IRAs), and pension accounts, among others. A ROTH IRA is a "tax free" account, which most young people qualify to own. Another kind of retirement savings is Social Security, which is an amount taken out of every paycheck you earn and saved by the federal government until you reach retirement age.

Quick Tips

- You should have your employer do automatic deductions from your paycheck directly into your retirement account. Shoot for at least 10-15% and you'll never even miss the money. Think of it as a tax, where you'll get a refund later.

- You can monitor this account with the same app you use to monitor your bank accounts, credit cards, budget, and other accounts. An overall picture of your net worth helps keep you on track.

For the most part these retirement assets accumulate during your working career. During your younger years, you're likely to invest these assets more aggressively than in your older years. A little risk can result in bigger gains. Plus, if you suffer a loss, you still have time to regain what you lost. As you approach retirement, you'll invest more conservatively to protect what you have.

Your bucket of retirement assets can get quite full and be a major component of your net worth and a large contributor to your retirement cash flow. Later in life, you'll work with a certified public accountant (CPA) or a financial planner to calculate distributions from these assets. A distribution is the amount the government requires you to withdraw from your assets every year. The amount is based on both your age and the balance in your retirement account.

Once you retire, the assets you have accumulated will replace the paychecks you earned during your working career. You will live off these assets. And that's why it's so important to start growing them now!

The different types of assets in this bucket grow and appreciate based on contributions you and your employers add (if your retirement plan includes an employer match), plus the annual growth in the value of the assets.

Now that your research is done, you should be ready to open your first retirement account. Perhaps it's a ROTH IRA or just a simple savings account until you have enough money to invest in retirement. It doesn't matter how you do it; the important thing is simply to take the first step. Think about retirement—and then act!

Personal Finance Stories

Kim signed up for her employer's 401(k) plan, and contributes 5% of her paycheck each time she receives one. She also clicked on the setting that allows her dividends and interest to be reinvested, which means that her money will grow even faster. She's able to monitor the portfolio from her mobile device at any time of the day or night, and she watches the ups and downs of the market carefully. But Kim is in it for the long haul and understands that there are days she might lose some money.

Over a 30-year period of investing 5% per month, reinvesting her dividends and interest, and pretty much leaving the account alone, the app projects a decent return - her account will be worth $1,186,253.14. If the stock market does even better than projected, it could be worth $2,129,907.44. And, if she were to save 10% per month, the portfolio would be worth $3,193,476.48. That's what happens to just a couple hundred dollars a month. As Kim's income grows, she'll be adding even more to the account.

Starting at this young age, Kim will be in great shape for a comfortable retirement.

Exercise: A Lifetime of Savings

Every Little Bit Counts

Making it a habit to save for retirement when you're young will have a huge impact on the quality of your life in your golden years! Unfortunately, many young people live for today and don't think about tomorrow. The exercise below demonstrates how just making modest contributions to your retirement account starting at age 25 could add up to millions of dollars for you to live on when you retire.

Exercise: Retirement Calculator

It's pretty hard to ignore the benefits of starting to save now! Unfortunately for many retirees, a time that should be joyful becomes a time of stress about how to afford their normal lifestyle as well as pay for doctors, medication and unexpected bills. Often, older folks have to find part-time jobs just to cover the cost of basic necessities and health insurance. basic food and health insurance. It doesn't have to be this way. Here's what can happen with some planning and good saving habits throuhgout your work life:

- Start saving at age 25.
- Contribute $10K per year into your retirement account from age 25-29.
- Contribute $18K per year into your retirement account from age 30-65.
- Withdraw $250K per year from age 66-93.
- At 7% growth, you'll have contributed only $700K, and can withdraw $7M with $2M leftover.
- For a healthy retirement, contribute 10% of your paycheck to your 401K until retirement and you should be in good shape.

AGE	BEG BALANCE	CONTRIBUTION	INTEREST	WITHDRAWAL	END BALANCE
25	$ -	$ 10,000.00	$ -		$ 10,000.00
26	$ 10,000.00	$ 10,000.00	$ 700.00		$ 20,700.00
27	$ 20,700.00	$ 10,000.00	$ 1,449.00		$ 32,149.00
28	$ 32,149.00	$ 10,000.00	$ 2,250.43		$ 44,399.43
29	$ 44,399.43	$ 10,000.00	$ 3,107.96		$ 57,507.39
30	$ 57,507.39	$ 18,000.00	$ 4,025.52		$ 79,532.91
31	$ 79,532.91	$ 18,000.00	$ 5,567.30		$ 103,100.21
32	$ 103,100.21	$ 18,000.00	$ 7,217.01		$ 128,317.23
33	$ 128,317.23	$ 18,000.00	$ 8,982.21		$ 155,299.43
66	$ 3,337,403.38	$ -	$ 233,618.24	$ 250,000.00	$ 3,321,021.61
67	$ 3,321,021.61	$ -	$ 232,471.51	$ 250,000.00	$ 3,303,493.13
92	$ 2,212,361.67		$ 154,865.32	$ 250,000.00	$ 2,117,226.99
93	$ 2,117,226.99		$ 148,205.89	$ 250,000.00	$ 2,015,432.88
		$ 698,000.00		$ 7,000,000.00	$ 9,015,432.88

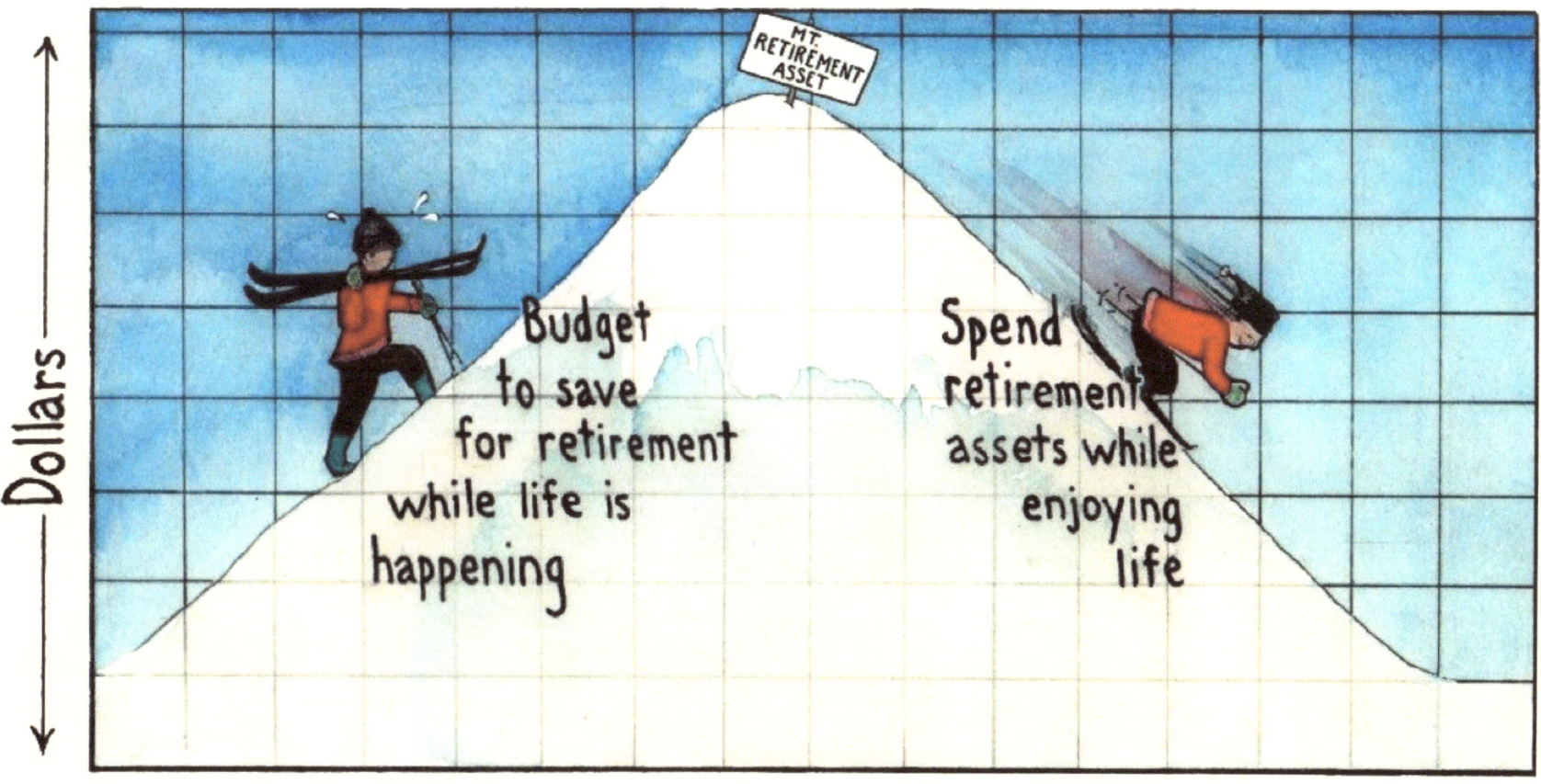

This is a simple way of looking at retirement savings. When you are a young adult, you start out with nothing and slowly nurture and build your own Mt. Retirement, which will amount to the money you need to have a fulfilling, stress-free retirement. As you reach retirement age, you should be reaching the top of the mountain, and if you've done everything correctly, it's as easy as skiing down the other side, enjoying the fruits of your labor.

Reading a Financial Statement

Why Do I Need To Know This?

If you want to be savvy when it comes to your finances, you need to know how to read and interpret a financial statement. To be savvy is to be smart, knowledgeable, and practical—all of which makes for good judgment. Many adults have trouble reading a financial statement—it's not easy to do. That's one reason to introduce you to it now. Another reason is to help you make better decisions when you pick stocks to buy or sell. The third reason relates to your future, which, as you know from the last chapter, begins now: if you have dreams of running your own business someday, you're eager to learn how. Reading a financial statement is a good place to start.

How Do I Get Started?

Start by looking up any company you're passionate about on the internet—maybe you buy their products or use their services. Maybe you like their mission, their commitment to a sustainable world, or their company culture. Whatever the reason, you want to know how they run. So, head to their stock symbol page and find their financials.

If you've ever read a nutrition label on the side of a cereal box, you know it lists things like the amount of fat, cholesterol, sugar, etc. That's really all that a financial statement is—it shows you where the money came from, where it went, and where it is now.

There are four types of financial statements: balance sheets, income statements, cash flow statements, and statements of shareholders' equity.

Balance Sheets (Point In Time)

These show what the company owns and what it owes at a fixed point in time. They provide information about the company's assets, liabilities, and shareholders' equity.

Assets are the goods that a company owns that have some kind of value and which can be sold. This could include a manufacturing plant, trucks, equipment, or inventor; it can also include intellectual property like trademarks and patents, cash and investments.

Liabilities are what the company owes to others. This could include loans from banks, rent for their building, payroll for employees, or taxes to the government.

Shareholders' equity is also known as capital or net worth, and is what would be left if the company sold all of its assets and paid off all of it's liabilities. The leftover money would go to the owners—also called shareholders.

These categories can be further broken into sub-categories, as you can see in our example, but for now we'll keep it simple. The formula

```
XYZ COMPANY
Balance Sheet
12/31/2017
```

ASSETS	
Current Assets:	
Cash	$12,000
Accounts Receivable	35,000
Inventory	120,000
Prepaid Rent	8,000
Total Current Assets	$175,000
Long-Term Assets	
Land	$126,000
Buildings & Improvements	300,000
Furniture & Fixtures	50,000
General Equipment	125,000
Total Fixed Assets	$601,000
TOTAL ASSETS	**$776,000**
LIABILITIES	
Current Liabilities:	
Accounts Payable	$60,000
Taxes Payable	25,000
Salaries/Wages Payable	30,000
Interest Payable	25,000
Total Current Liabilities	$140,000
Long Term Liabilities:	
Loan 1	$322,000
Total Long Term Liabilities	$322,000
TOTAL LIABILITIES	**$462,000**
OWNER'S EQUITY	
Paid in Capital	$64,000
Retained Earnings	250,000
TOTAL OWNER'S EQUITY	**$314,000**
TOTAL LIABILITIES & OWNER'S EQUITY	**$776,000**

to remember is that **assets = liabilities + equity**. The balance sheet is set up the same way—first assets, then liabilities, and finally owner's equity.

Income Statement (Over A Period of Time)

Another kind of financial statement is the income statement, which shows how much money (called revenue) a company made over a period of time, like over the course of a year. In addition to the total revenue, you'll also be able to find out the costs and expenses associated with earning that revenue. Finally, at the bottom of the statement, you'll see how much the company earned or lost during that period of time—called the net earnings or net losses.

Reading an income statement is pretty straightforward. At the top, you'll see the income, or revenue, from sales. As you move down the statement, you'll see a list of expenses, which are subtracted from the income. Be sure to look up the definition of words you don't know, like amortization and depreciation.

Cash Flow Statement

As it states, this reports shows the flow of cash in and out of the company. It tells us whether or not the company has enough cash on hand to pay its expenses and to purchase assets. It does this

INCOME STATEMENT
For the Years Ending December 31, 2017

REVENUES:	
Sales Revenue	$500,000
Other Revenue	$0
(Less Sales Returns & Allowances	0
TOTAL REVENUES	**$500,000**
Cost of Goods Sold	150,000
GROSS PROFIT	**$350,000**
EXPENSES:	
Accounting	$2,500
Advertising	25,000
Amortization	0
Bad Debt	1,000
Depreciation	50,000
Employee Payroll Tax	15,000
Employee Wages	100,000
Entertainment	0
Insurance	2,000
Interest Expense	12,000
Miscellaneous	5,000
Rent	24,000
Software	0
Telephone	2,500
Utilities	7,000
Web Hosting	500
Vehicle Expense	12,000
-	0
-	0
-	0
-	0
TOTAL EXPENSES	**$258,500**
NET INCOME BEFORE TAXES	**$91,500**
Less Income Tax Expense	0
NET INCOME	**$91,500**

by combining details from the balance sheet with details from the income statement to show cash flow over time. The details are organized into three categories: operating activities, investing activities and financing activities.

Operating activities includes all activities that bring money into the company or spend money to keep the company operating. If money is owed to the company, called Accounts receivable, parentheses are placed around the amount owed. Money the company owes for expenses, are called Accounts payable and are also shown with parentheses around the amount.

Investing activities shows cash flow related to investment the company has made, like the purchase or sale of a piece of property, equipment or piece of machinery. Purchases would require an outflow of cash; seling an investment would create an inflow of cash.

Financing activities shows cash flow from selling stocks and bonds or from borrowing money from banks.

Cash from Operating Activities	
Earnings	$248
Depreciation	$239
Accounts receivable	($108)
Inventory	$244
Current assets	($18)
Accounts payable	($107)
Cash from Operations	**$498**
Cash from Investing Activities	
Property, plant, & Equipment	($205)
Other long-term assets	$20
Cash from Investing	**($185)**
Cash from Financing Activities	
Credit line	($50)
Current portion of long term debt	$1
Long-term debt	($121)
Other long-term liabilities	$34
Equity (dividend)	($166)
Cash from Financing	**($302)**
Change in Cash	$11
Cash at Beginning	$72
Cash at End	**$83**

At the bottom of the report, you'll learn a key fact about the company: how much cash does it have in hand. In other words, is it making a profit or is it in debt? Being comfortable reading these kinds of reports is a big deal and a big step in financial growth. As with everything in this process, ask questions, do your research, and don't give up!

Making a Good Impression

Why Do I Need To Know This?

There's still a lot more to learn on your journey into adulthood and beyond. Believe it or not, the learning process is much easier if you establish a good relationship with the people you meet on your journey—your banker, your first boss, your teachers and college professors—all the different people you'll meet along the way. Making a good impression on these kinds of people is an important first step in building good and lasting relationships. Many of these people will be your mentors and advocates—they will become part of your network, introducing you to their contacts, helping you get a job, giving you a good reference. Your network will be your lifeline throughout your career. And it starts with a rock-solid first impression. It's really the difference between being ordinary and being extraordinary.

How Do I Get Started?

Getting started is as easy as paying attention to successful people around you. What do you notice about them that makes them stand out? You can also watch videos online that demonstrate things like how to tie a tie, tipping etiquette, table manners, and what a good handshake looks and feels like. Here are a few key pointers:

- **A firm handshake:** There is nothing worse than shaking a limp hand. Instead, make eye contact, reach out your right hand, and shake the other person's right hand with a firm grip. A confident handshake earns major

Quick Tips

- Treat people the way you want them to treat you. It's an old saying, but still holds up.

- When interviewing, take a little extra time to get a haircut, iron your clothes, arrive a little early, and be prepared. Often, the person who makes the best impression gets the job.

- When it comes to personal finance, making a good impression is a big part of building relationships, which can lead to better business opportunities and ultimately making more money.

points toward a good impression.

- **Dress for success:** When going for a first interview, always wear "business professional" clothes unless otherwise instructed. Shine your dress shoes, iron your shirt and pants, dress or skirt, and pay attention to the details—remember a belt, socks, understated earrings, etc. Never wear shorts, a tee-shirt, or flip flops to an interview. Caring about the way you look shows that you are serious and respectful of both the interviewer and the job you want.

- **Personal grooming:** Much like dressing for success, always make sure your appearance represents you at your best. That means neatly trimmed hair and fingernails, perfume or aftershave that isn't overpowering, and a polished look overall.

- **Confidence:** Speak with confidence! You might want to practice ahead of time. It's always good to have a few topics you're comfortable discussing so that when you're in social situations, you can keep a conversation going. Also, stand up straight, with your shoulders back, and make eye contact with whoever is speaking to you. Show interest in what they are saying and be ready to ask questions.

- **Table manners:** Knowing how to properly use a knife, fork, and spoon is a good start, but what do you do when you have three forks, three spoons and two knives? Make sure you know which is for salad, soups, or the main course and how to hold them properly. Place your napkin in your lap, don't speak with your mouth full of food, and eat slowly enough to participate in conversations during the meal.

- **Tipping:** There are plenty of online guides as to how much you should tip different people, but the rule of thumb for a restaurant meal is to double the tax listed on the bill and add a little bit more. Also, make sure you leave tips for hotel staff, shuttle bus drivers and others who do you a service.

- **Always be courteous:** When opening a door, hold it open for the person coming in behind you. It's the right thing to do. Treat service staff with respect, from the janitor to the waitress to the receptionist. They are doing their jobs and don't need your bad attitude. Also, don't start eating until everyone's food has arrived at the table. And never start to eat before your host/hostess does. Bad manners make a very big impression!

There's a story of a boss who would interview prospective employees at a restaurant for breakfast. He'd arrive a few minutes early and offer a generous tip to the staff if they would agree to screw up the order of the potential hire and make a few other mistakes. How the potential hire handled the situation would determine whether or not he or she got the job. Treating everyone respectfully, especially in difficult circumstances, makes a big difference.

Taking time to make a good impression will make your journey a whole lot easier, shorter, and more successful. It doesn't take much effort to learn these basics, but it takes discipline to turn them into good habits. Go for it!

How to talk to my parents about finances

Some people feel very comfortable discussing finances with their family, and others cringe at the idea. But it is an important and necessary conversation for all parents and guardians to have with their children, especially when it comes to after high school. Will you be completely independent after high school or will your family still support you? If you go to college, what will you be expected to contribute to cover tuition, room, board and extra expenses? Based on how the conversation goes, you can plan accordingly. It's much better to know in advance than to be surprised at the last minute. And, if you need to get a job right after high school graduation, you'll have time to find one you really want. Honestly, it's a great idea to at least help out with your expenses after high school—it will definitely give you a sense of independence and responsibility—two of the most important qualities for financial success?

Another important topic to discuss with your family is insurance. How long are they willing and/or able to keep you on their policy? In other words, do you need to get your own policy? This conversation might be able to wait a couple years, but it is still important to keep in mind.

Other topics to discuss include student loans for college, setting up a retirement account, and investing in the stock market—all topics you have been introduced to in this book. If you tell your parent or guardian that you are interested in talking about family finances as they relate to you, it's likely they will listen! Don't be afraid to ask. These are important topics for your future, and the only way to develop a plan is to know how, when and where to start. Family support of your goals is crucial!

~ Part Two: Something For Everyone ~

5 Buckets, 4 Shovels, a Beach and a Map is a simplified approach to financial planning that uses drawings, charts, and examples to help give anyone at any age plan for their financial future. The Buckets, the Shovels, the Beach and the Map are all metaphors for the various aspects of financial planning. The drawings and charts are easy to understand and follow. For young adults, this approach integrates all of the topics we've discussed and integrating them into one big financial plan.

For most adults, the idea of linking tax funds, retirement savings, cash flow, insurance, an estate plan, and investments can be frightening and confusing. It seems like a long, complicated process and, as a result, most people have a difficult time getting started.

Our approach—5 Buckets, 4 Shovels, a Beach and a Map—makes financial security a visual process and creates a systematic approach that will protect you from sudden misfortunes and help you save for a rewarding retirement. We describe it in-depth a book by the same name, but we'll give you a brief overview in the next few pages.

Although these topics may seem completely unrelated to a young person's life, it's very helpful to learn about the big picture now. It will make all the little pieces of the picture much easier to figure out later. By starting with retirement, we hope to inspire students to include this key factor in their financial plan right from the start.

~ Introducing the Buckets, Shovels, Beach and Map ~

The Buckets

As you can see, each of the buckets is of a different shape and size. This makes sense because the asset groups that each bucket represents are all very different. Assets groups are the way we categorize our financial products, which you will acquire during your life. With a little imagination and some organization, you will see that every asset can be placed into one of the five buckets. Think about all the ideas we've already talked about and how they might fit into each of these buckets.

Liquid Assets Bucket

These are the assets that you can save and spend frequently with little or no tax effect. This is also where you would deposit your paycheck and pay your living expenses. Basically, this bucket contains your checking, savings account and liquid investments that are not tax deferred (retirement accounts are tax deferred).

Insurance Assets Bucket

These are the insurance assets and products that you will need throughout your lifetime. These include term life insurance, whole life insurance, and disability insurance, as well as property, casualty, and general liability insurance.

Personal Assets Bucket

These are the physical assets that you own, such as your house, a second home, your car, your jewelry, and other valuable items. Often these assets include a loan or mortgage (for instance, for a car or a house).

Retirement Assets Bucket

These are the assets that are accumulating on a tax deferred basis, and they are specifically for your retirement. These include IRAs, pension plans, 401(k) accounts, and social security.

Investment Assets Bucket

These are long-term assets such as rental real estate, your company, or possibly an inheritance that you expect to receive. The hope is that these assets will appreciate over time and will generate a large amount of cash when it comes time to liquidate them—to sell them.

The Shovels

The shovels represent the experts who have the training and experience to guide you through the ongoing process of most efficiently filling and emptying the buckets at the right time. Right now, you probably don't need to worry much about having advisors, but as you get older, and start to accumulate more "stuff", you'll need knowledgable people who can help you manage it all so you don't make costly mistakes. The shovels are:

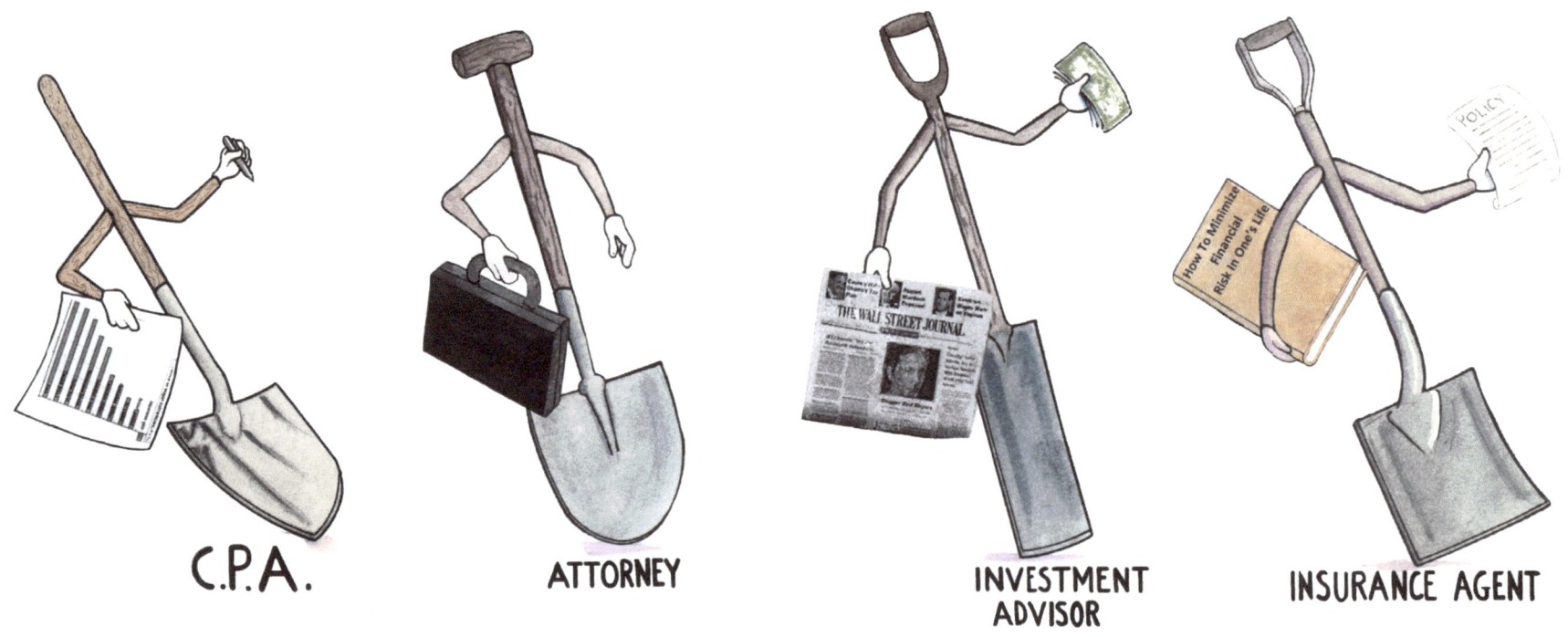

Your CPA Shovel

This expert is usually an accountant, and handles your taxes and helps you manage your money. People who have a lot of money usually need help managing it all so that they don't spend too much, can afford all of the things they want to buy and still have funds for an emergency and retirement. The CPA is also the person who helps manage all of the other experts.

Your Attorney Shovel

This expert handles all of the legal paperwork related to your finances. Ask your parents if they have a will or trust, or estate plan (if they don't, you might want to gently nudge them to do this!) If they do, they probably hired an attorney to help them with all the paperwork. If they have ever bought and/or sold a house, they had to work with a lawyer to complete the legal documents. Lawyers are indispensable.

Your Investment Shovel

This expert handles your investments, guiding you to make informe decisions about what to invest in and how to diversify your investments (so that you don't put all your money in one place). This person will also help you buy and sell your investments when you're likely to make money and to prevent you from losing it. He or she is likely to manage your retirement funds too.

Your Insurance Shovel

This expert takes care of your insurance, which covers you in case of an accident, injury or death. There are all kinds of insurance, like car insurance, medical insurance, homeowners insurance, life insurance, etc. You usually pay a monthly fee for ongoing coverage. Most people have several different insurance policies.

The Beach

The beach represents your life, including all of the people that you will meet, the gradual evolution that will take place in life, and also the sudden and dramatic changes (huge storms) that we all will face. The pictures below begins with a couple living their lives contently, and then a storm hits and washes the beach away. In real life, these storms include things such as losing a job, losing a home, illness, or hospitalization, divorce, or the death of a family member. All of these storms create a financial crisis. But, when the storm ends, life eventually goes back to some degree of normalcy, just like the third picture of the beach below. Life makes the planning process more complicated but more interesting! A good financial plan will try to account for the storms and the renewal that occurs afterwards. The couple below had children, which they accounted for in their financial plan. No wonder they look happy!

The sand on the beach represents your money. Over the course of your life, the shovels (your advisors) will help you fill the various buckets with sand (money) and eventually work with you to move sand from one bucket to another when it's appropriate to do so.

The Map

The Map represents the plan that will help guide you to achieve financial security. The plan will constantly change as you meander through life, but the outcome should lead you to your well-earned pot o'gold. Flexibility is key and staying on track is paramount.

The Shovels Working Together

For the financial plan to work, it requires a lot of teamwork among the four shovels. The scene to the left shows advisors, together with the family, reviewing the map and tweaking the plan as needed. It's very important to understand that success depends on cooperation to create and then regularly adjust your long term plan.

Let's look at several features of the illustration:

First, it shows the whole family being involved in the process. Often, parents don't get their children involved at an early enough age. Of course, this is a family decision, but the right time to start this process is sooner rather than later.

Second, it shows the advisors working together. Too often the advisors work in a vacuum, which causes them to give the client competing and conflicting advice.

Third, there is an empty chair. This represents the rest of the advisors—bankers, real estate agents, consultants—that may be needed from time to time. There should always be room for them.

Fourth, the picture shows everyone using the same map—only one map—and adjusting and tweaking it as life (the beach) dictates.

This combination—the entire family working together with all the advisors on the same map—is a powerful strategy with a high likelihood of success.

~ Part Three: Building Your Own Plan ~

We have now explained the concepts behind *5 Buckets, 4 Shovels, a Beach and a Map*. We have discussed popular financial topics that young adults should know. Now, we will give you practical advice and show you how to put these concepts into practice at different stages of your life.

Learning about financial security and applying that throughout your life is a constant development. You will always be changing as will your finances. As you grow, your knowledge of personal finance will grow as well. Don't be too worried if it seems overwhelming now. For now, here are some steps you can take within the first few years as you begin on your path to financial security.

Keep in mind that everyone's path is different. The ages in the chart to the left are simply a general timeline. You can, and should, do everything at your own pace and when you see fit. Don't feel constrained by these specific ages and tasks—they are presented here to help you give a broad picture of what young adults can be thinking about when it comes to personal finance.

~ Adulting Milestones ~

AGES 13-15	AGES 16-18	AGES 19-21	AGES 21-25
Bring up the topic of finances with your parent or guardian	Open a personal checking and/or savings account	Adjust your budget according to any new financial situations, like a new job, more expenses, owning a car	Add student loans into budget and begin to pay them off
Begin researching banks, credit cards, etc.	Create a monthly budget	Figure out if you need to work or get student loans for college	Learn about various insurance policies and what you need
Don't stress—you're just researching.	Receive your first debit or credit card	Continue paying off your car loan and building a good credit history	Do your own taxes (where you need to use your W-2, bank documents, college documents, etc.)
	If you are planning on getting a car, begin researching loans		Invest in the stock market
	If you are working part-time, save your W-2 form		Start your retirement fund (401k, IRA, etc.) and invest at least 10%

~ What's Next ~

Things You Should Consider at Every Stage of Your Life and Career

- Make sure you update the plan every year. Some parts of the plan it can be updated every five years.

- If you use credit cards, try to pay off the balance every month. Use the automatic payment option.

- Create a budget of your expected incomes and expenses. The budget should include savings for specific goals such as college, a second home, a big vacation.

- The budget should have short-term goals, like three years, as well as a long term focus on your needs for retirement funds.

- Create an estate plan that designates where your assets go if you and/or your significant other were to die suddenly. Make sure assets are in trusts and things are properly documented. Writing down your wishes to explain the estate plan is a good idea.

- If possible, own your home. You build equity every month and in the long run it is less expensive than renting.

- Save for retirement every month without fail. If possible, use the Roth feature for retirement funds.

- Protect your family with well-thought-out life insurance policies. Depending on your circumstances, consider both term and permanent insurance.

- Use your advisors. No one fills their own cavities or cuts their own hair. Your advisors are there to guide you. Assuming you have the right advisors and your plan is well-coordinated, the cost for advisors is minor compared to the benefits received.

- Share your plan with your family (especially your kids) at the appropriate age.

- Think about non-profits and charities that you can about and the legacy you want to leave behind.

- Don't live your plan for your heirs, and don't live your life in such a frugal way that you don't enjoy the benefits of your hard work throughout your life.

Building Your Own Financial Plan

What are the most important aspects of your life right now? Think about friends, family, extracurricular activities, school, work, etc. How will you create your financial plan and budget around these key features?

_____

_____

According to the chart on page 100, what age range are you in? What steps should you be taking right now to ensure your future financial security?

_____

_____

How will you communicate your financial plan to the people who are important to you?

_____

_____

Financial goals are likely to change over time. Earlier in life you might be planning to buy a car, applying for your first credit card or save for college. Later in life, you might be more interested in travel, retirement, and charitable giving. What are your financial goals today, both short term and long term?

_____

_____

What are your interests? Maybe you like to volunteer or want to travel. Putting money aside to fund your interests as well as fun activities, like vacations, should be part of your overall financial plan.

_____

_____

Values play a big part in creating a financial plan that will work for your lifetime. For some people, their family and friends are of highest value; for others, it's their church and volunteering their time. What are your values?

_____

_____

What is the first tangible step you will take today in order to move your financial plan forward? Examples could be choosing the bank where you will open an account today or figuring out what type of credit card you will apply for. Even if it is a small step, take it!

_____

_____

Use the following pages to map out your next steps, to write an example budget, to figure out your car loans, which stocks to invest in. Your financially successful future can begin here and now!

_____

_____

_____

_____

_____

_____

~ The 5 Bucket 4 Shovel Foundation ~

Supporting Financial Literacy in Young Adults

When we released our first book, *5 Buckets, 4 Shovels, a Beach and a Map*, we quickly found that many of our adult clients were handing that book over to their kids to learn a little more about financial security and managing their money. At the same time, we kept hearing about high school students who were entering college without the basic knowledge of personal finance. College is a time of great change for these kids—usually moving out on their own for the first time, dealing with students loans and managing their budgets. We knew this group needed help and that we were in a position to provide the help.

The foundation's mission is to provide financial literacy support for young adults heading into adulthood. All profits from both of our books go directly to the foundation to purchase these books, which are then provided free of charge to schools and young adults. Donations to the foundation also come from our corporate sponsors. All books are available through Amazon.com. Support the foundation at https://www.5buckets4shovels.com/.

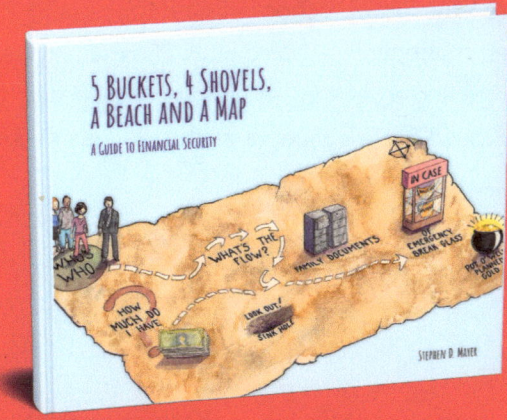

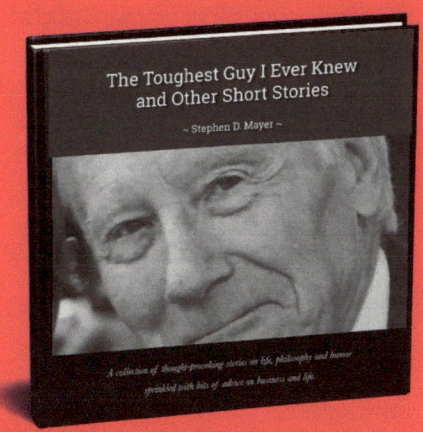

About the Artist: Richard Sigberman

Born in New York City in 1952, Richard began drawing at an early age and loved it. Rich became serious about fine art and illustration in college, but he is mostly self-taught. He also studied at the NYC Art Students League for 18 months.

Rich was a newspaper illustrator for the Palo Alto Times Tribune from 1983-87, responsible for creating images for the business section.

Since then, Richard has been a free-lance illustrator and fine artist, having created many posters, jazz-oriented art, personal celebration pieces and, most recently, a 25-page sequential art story based on a Nigerian legend. Rich feels that the work he did for Steve Mayer was exemplary in that it combined Steve's ideas and good writing, with his ability to distill that into images that both illuminate and attract the reader, and makes the copy more inviting. Early on in this project, he told Steve, "I feel I was born to do this kind of art".

About the Author: Stephen D. Mayer

Stephen D. Mayer was born in San Francisco in 1954, where he attended Riordan High School and then U.C. Berkeley.

A CPA by trade, Steve's entrepreneurial nature has lead him to be involved in starting more than 18 different businesses.

He lives in San Mateo with his wife, Patty, of over 25 years and has three children—Dylan, and twins, Kenzie and Nicola.

Steve is a man of many traditions, including over 40 consecutive years of backpacking with his group of friends. For fun, when he turned 60, he completed an Ironman "because it seemed like a worthy goal."

Steve also enjoys writing, especially when his experiences can help someone else. This book was written to help fill in the gaps where students are leaving high school without the personal finance knowledge they need to function — basic stuff, like reading a paycheck, filing taxes or getting a car loan. He hopes this will help them understand some of these basic concepts as they move into adulthood.

www.ingramcontent.com/pod-product-compliance
Lightning Source LLC
Chambersburg PA
CBHW050854010526

44118CB00004BA/165